بِسْمِ اللهِ الرَّحْمٰنِ الرَّحِيْمِ

In the name of Allah, the Most Gracious,
the Most Merciful.

Praise for National Parks and the Remembrance of Allah

"Abeer's book uniquely delves into how to use creation to remember our ultimate Creator. Abeer beautifully masters reflecting on our faith by observing the world around us, from vast mountains and canyons to the most intricate flower. As someone who greatly connects to Allah through nature, I was deeply moved by this work. The photographs of the national parks are just as beautiful as the words. Highly recommend this read for anyone yearning to draw nearer to Allah."

- Shaziya Barkat - Author of My Iman Journal

"There are so many national parks that I have on my list to visit and Abeer's book added a strong spiritual motivation to pursue witnessing these spectacular sites. Verses of the Quran and weaved through the text and it was incredible to see how often Allah tells us to look at what He created- as signs. This book takes you on a spiritual journey through the national parks. Even the illustrations were wonderful."

- Naimah Abraham, Author of In the Belly of the Whale

"Through her book, Abeer takes you on a spectacular voyage through nature, in all its magnificence. Her creativity and insightfulness are evidently manifest in how eloquently she connects what she witnesses of God's creation, in the National Parks of the USA, with verses from the Qur'an, as well as narrations from the Prophet Muhammad (peace be upon him). It is rare to find a body of writing that so powerfully links the Creator with His creation - but my goodness, Abeer has accomplished this. If you are looking for a pathway by which you can connect more deeply with your Lord, then you have found it, insha'Allah."

- Kashmir Maryam, Author of The Muslim Woman's Manifesto

NATIONAL PARKS AND THE REMEMBRANCE OF ALLAH ﷻ

A Muslim's journey through the National Parks to remember Allah ﷻ and the Prophets

ABEER ARAIN

Illustrations by Ashley Limbaugh

Nature Chronicles Press

Library of Congress Cataloging-in-Publishing Data Names: Arain, Abeer
Title: National Parks and the remembrance of Allah / Abeer Arain
Description: First Edition. Nature Chronicles Press, 2022
Identifiers: LCCN 2022914283

Nature Chronicles Press

ISBN: 979 – 8 – 9866990 – 0 – 4 (hardback)
ISBN: 979 – 8 – 9866990 – 1– 1 (paperback)
ISBN: 979 – 8- 9866990 – 2 – 8 (ebook)
Copyediting by Cyrus McGoldrick
Cover design by Abeer Arain & Sheeba Sheikh
Arabic calligraphy vectors by Waqar Asim
Illustrations by Ashley Limbaugh
Book Design by Jessica Cameron

To Shaykh Mufti Taqi Usmani.

*His teachings changed
the way I look at nature.*

*He is Allah, the Creator, the Inventor, the Shaper. His are
the Most Beautiful Names. His purity is proclaimed by all
that is in the heavens and the earth, and He is the
All-Mighty, the All-Wise."*

(Al-Hashr 59:24)

Contents

NATIONAL PARKS AND THE

REMEMBRANCE

OF ALLAH ﷻ

Foreword

*I (Allah) did not create the jinns and the human beings
except that they should worship me…*

(Al-Dhāriyāt 51:56)

The lockdowns of the COVID pandemic were a wake-up
call. Many of us were reminded of the importance of spending
time in nature and exploring the outdoors. Many families are
more likely now to get together for cross-country travel and
camping. Our time seems too short to take full advantage of
the endless opportunities available to us outdoors.

One way to begin exploring the natural treasures of any country is to visit its national parks. Let's take the example of the United States, where I live. There are sixty-three national parks here, some of which are amongst the world's most sought-after vacation destinations. They have been designated to protect and preserve diverse wildlife in its natural habitat, scenic landscapes of mountains and waterfalls, and distinctive geological marvels that make these parks home to some of the planet's most fascinating landmarks.

For a Muslim, traveling to a national park is not just an item on a bucket list, but rather an opportunity to praise the magnificence of Allah ﷻ and to reflect on our eventual departure from this world.

The mutual rivalry (for piling up of worldly things) distracts you, until you reach the graves.

(Al-Takāthur 102:1-2)

Allah ﷻ has blessed many of us with the strength to explore the world and observe His creation, so that we can learn from it and prepare for our *akhirah,* the hereafter. We are blessed with countless favors from our Creator, and one way to bring our hearts closer to Him is by the *dhikr* (remembrance) of His blessings. Everything in nature can bring us closer to Allah ﷻ if we pay close attention to it. Traveling through the national parks is an opportunity to praise the majestic beauty that He created. We can either visit the Yellowstone National Park for fun and diversion, or we can observe it with the eyes of faith, *imān*, and use our journey as a reminder to repent and to rectify our actions before death approaches us.

This book is not a travel guide, per se, but rather it was written to bring our attention to the greatest benefit of exploring the outdoors. I have always been an avid traveler, and I loved visiting the national parks, just to explore and hike the trails and admire the beauty of the mountains. But then Allah ﷻ blessed me with new perspective, especially through the thoughtful speeches of Shaykh Mufti Taqi Usmani, on the opportunity provided by spending time in nature. I started to see the natural habitat around me differently. I learned that the meadows, forests, and trails around us can be not only sources of enjoyment and education but also opportunities to earn great rewards by praising the One who designed and created this beautiful world for us. With this perspective, my exploration of nature made me feel closer to Allah ﷻ and refreshed in my *imān*.

National Parks and the Remembrance of Allah ﷻ takes us on a journey through the national parks in the United States and connects us with reminders from the Qur'an and the stories of the prophets. Although this book is inspired specifically by the U.S. national parks, the idea can be applied anywhere, and the real aim is to bring our attention toward the *dhikr* of Allah while observing nature.

Say, "Look at what there is in the heavens and the earth." But signs and warnings do not suffice people who do not believe.
(Yūnus 10:101)

Letter from the Author

Dear reader,

Before we start our journey through the national parks, I would like to draw your attention to the objective of this book. As I have mentioned earlier, this book is not a travel guide, therefore it does not list any routes of the hiking trails or camping areas. The purpose of this short book is to direct the attention of the reader towards the remembrance of Allah ﷻ and recall our prophets – their lifestyle, hardships, and consciousness of Allah's presence – while we enjoy the outdoors. Today we sometimes hear about concepts like "forest-bathing" and "retreat in the woods", and nowadays we see more people getting out in nature and exploring the backcountry. However, the feeling of wholeness in nature is incomplete without the *dhikr* of the One who created it. Taking a walk in the woods ("vitamin N") may provide healing for our bodies and minds, but the soul finds its harmonious balance only with the remembrance of Allah ﷻ.

Bring this book with you on your next journey and you may find it helpful in connecting nature with the *dhikr* of Allah ﷻ. For example, when looking at an enormous tree, think about the massive root system and how Allah ﷻ provides nutrition to the trees regardless of whether they live in fertile soil or thrive on the rocky hills. When walking in the forest, notice the ground layer of our ecosystem. Observe the impressive diversity in the colors, patterns, and forms of different leaves and shrubs, all of which tell us about the Divine Glory of Allah ﷻ, the Sustainer of the entire universe. The goal is to motivate you to think about Allah's magnificent planning when it comes to our planet's exquisite landscapes so the next time you appreciate any scenic beauty, you observe it through the lens of *imān*. Going out in the woods not only offers a golden opportunity for *dhikr* but also provides valuable time to make *dua* and ask Allah for whatever your heart desires. After all, the most important relationship we have is our connection with Allah ﷻ.

I also would like to recommend that instead of reading this book from start to finish, begin with your favorite component in nature, such as the trees, mountains, volcanoes, or animals. At the end of this book, I have also included a list of other books in the bibliography section that can be a good resource for anyone interested in learning more about nature and the national parks.

Lastly, my goal for writing this book will be achieved if my book inspires you to remember Allah on your next hiking trip. This would mean more to me than having this book on any bestseller chart of this fleeting world.

I hope you enjoy your time as a dendrophile (someone who loves trees and forests), and the next time you go for a hike, I pray that you feel the enchantment of the *dhikr* by the plants and trees around you. I hope you too join them in remembering the Most Compassionate, the Most Merciful. I wish you the best of luck in your travel endeavors.

Sincerely,

Abeer,
by the Stehekin River, North Cascades National Park

1

Travel and Dhikr of Allah ﷻ

And among His signs (is this), that you see the earth barren,
but when We send down water (rain) to it, it is stirred to
life and growth (of vegetation). Verily, He Who gives it life,

> *surely, (He) is Able to give life to the dead (on the Day of Resurrection). Indeed! He is Able to do all things.*
>
> *(Al-Fussilāt 41:39)*

`A`'ishah ﵂ narrated that the Prophet ﷺ used to remember Allah in all his affairs (Tirmidhī 3384).

Imagine a group of people stopping to look at a beautiful landscape. Everyone is delighted to see the beauty of nature. Some get busy capturing the best view on their cameras, others are looking for even more scenic viewpoints. While the crowd is checking off an item from their bucket lists, one person observing the picturesque mountains is admiring the creative power of Allah ﷻ. While others are busy thinking about how to acquire more worldly attention, this person is remembered in the gathering of angels, because as the Prophet ﷺ said, "No people gather to remember Allah but that the angels surround them, cover them with mercy, send tranquility upon them, and mention them to Allah among those near to Him." (Muslim 2700)

The *dhikr* (remembrance) of Allah ﷻ is not limited to any specific place. Allah ﷻ can and should be remembered anytime, anywhere, whether one is lying in bed or standing on a mountain. His *dhikr* is not even dependent on the tongue but can be done silently in the heart as well. All it takes is a heart that is blessed with the remembrance of Allah ﷻ. Many of us today get caught up in the technology of modern society, focused on advancing in a career or other social standing. The race to attain the trappings of this lower world (*dunya*) might then rob us of the greatest joy, the joy of observing the details in the creations of Allah ﷻ and being grateful for *hidāyah* (guidance). Our beloved Prophet ﷺ once said to his companions, "The best action that raises our rank, purest in the sight of Allah, and better than spending gold and silver, is the remembrance of Allah" (Tirmidhī).

Everything on our planet contains another world of intricate details within it. From the unique anatomy of ants to the intricate pattern of each snowflake, there is complexity in everything that testifies to the greatness of Allah. In the Holy Qur'an, Allah ﷻ urges us to travel and observe the system of this world and acknowledge how well it is controlled by the supreme power of Allah ﷻ.

Do they not, then, travel on earth so that they will have hearts to understand with, or ears to listen with? Verily, it is not the eyes that turn blind, but what turns blind is the hearts contained in the chests.

(Al-Ḥajj 46)

The remembrance of Allah ﷻ is one of the primary differentiating factors between a believer and a non-believer. Our Prophet ﷺ taught us supplications for every facet of our daily life, for things as mundane as entering the bathroom. The purpose of this is to maintain a close connection with the Most Merciful. The *dhikr* of Allah ﷻ reminds us of our inevitable departure from this world, the return to our Creator. *Alhamdulillah*, we remember Allah in our everyday life through *salah* (prayer), fasting, and *duā* (supplication), but unfortunately, we are often distracted from His *dhikr* by our work and travels. Sometimes the travel is to achieve purely materialistic goals, looking for our serenity in the satisfaction of worldly desires, when the truest peace comes only with the remembrance of Allah 🕮.

Those who believe (in the Oneness of Allah) and whose hearts are peaceful with the remembrance of Allah. Verily, in the remembrance of Allah do hearts find peace.

(Ar-Ra'd 13:28)

Someone once asked me, "What is the point of exploring nature when it all looks the same?" This kind of thinking might lead to a deeper ingratitude towards the blessings around us. For a believer, there are signs of Allah's glory everywhere, including the bounties of nature. And anyway, despite some similarities by category, the natural elements hardly look the same at all. Even a local city park might have more than a dozen types of fronds and florets. In the same way, the mountains around the Grand Canyon are remarkably different than the Cascades or the Alps. Isn't it amazing that there are uncountable mountains and waterfalls and species of trees, flowers, and shrubs on our planet? And the Creator of all of them is One, Allah 🕮!

Traveling in nature without remembering its Creator is like living in a room with no roof. No matter how much we fill the room with luxuries – money, shopping, travel, etc. – the room will always feel empty without the protection and closure of a roof, the consciousness of the presence of Allah ﷻ. Our Prophet ﷺ once mentioned: "The house where Allah is remembered and the house where He is not are like the living and the dead." (Muslim 779)

Today we know more than ever about the mountains, the depths of the oceans, and the geological details of everything in between. But if that knowledge does not strengthen our connection with Allah ﷻ it will prove to be a waste of our time and resources. Whether hiking a trail or sitting beside a river, our heart can be directed towards Allah ﷻ with the *dhikr* of His Majesty and *shukr* (gratitude) for His blessings. The more we reflect on the favors of Allah ﷻ, the more we admire His unparalleled glory. According to one *hadith qudsi*, the Prophet ﷺ said that Allah said, "I am as My slave thinks of Me, and I am with him when he remembers Me. If he remembers Me to himself, I remember him to Myself, and if he remembers Me in a gathering, I remember him in a gathering better than that.

And if he seeks to draw nearer to Me by a hand span, I draw nearer to him by a forearm's length, and if he comes to Me walking, I come to him with speed." (Tirmidhī 3603)

Let's begin our journey with some of the prominent features of our natural world. We will be exploring some of the national parks in the U.S., but the idea of closely observing nature and connecting it with the remembrance of Allah 🌸 can be applied anywhere in the world.

"O Allah, help me remember You, be grateful to You, and worship You in an excellent manner."

(Abu Dawud)

2

The Trees

Is it you who has originated its tree, or are We

the originator?

(Al-Wāqiʿah 56:72)

Standing tall and obeying Allah ﷻ throughout their lives, trees are silent living beings with entire universes inside them. Starting as tiny seedlings they soon break through the soil and steadily rise upwards. Allah ﷻ has made the trees with such complexity that scientists still do not completely understand their behavior. Compared to some of the other parts of nature, like geysers, waterfalls, and mountains, trees might feel the most alive to us. When it comes to the trees of the national parks, the two unique varieties of trees find their home in California. These are the coast redwoods and the giant sequoias.

Coast redwoods are the tallest tree on our planet, and they begin from seeds as tiny as those of tomatoes. They can weigh up to 500 tons and reach up to 380 feet. They are among the fastest-growing trees on earth and can grow up to three to ten feet per year. Most redwoods achieve their vertical growth within the first hundred years of their life. Not far from the redwoods at Redwood National Park are the sequoia trees of Sequoia National Park. Sequoias are not as tall as redwoods, growing up to 311 feet, but they are amongst the oldest trees on earth, about 3200 years old, which means they were blessed to be on the planet during the time of our beloved Prophet ﷺ.

The giant sequoias are the largest trees in the entire world. Their roots are barely ten to thirteen feet deep but cover an area of up to sixty to eight feet. Trees are social beings and help each other in a kind of community. Their roots host a large population of fungi that connect them with each other and transmit information about dangers like drought or insects. It is a sign of the mastery of Allah ﷻ that He created such unique flora that stand quietly in the ground yet communicate with everything in their surroundings, *subhānallah*.

When hiking in the forest, take a moment to notice the leaves of a tree. Each tree contains a certain pattern on its leaves with a similar structure. Some trees, like the Hopp tree, might even change the shape of their leaves as they mature.

If all the trees on earth become pens, and the sea replenished by seven more seas were to supply them with ink, yet the Words of Allah would not be exhausted. Verily, Allah is All- Mighty, All-Wise.

(Luqmān 31:27)

The world of trees is so deep that botanists and foresters have written hundreds, maybe thousands of books about them. To-day, scientists are discovering that trees also have a sense of smell, and they even feel painful stimuli.

Have you not seen that whoever is in the heavens and who-ever is on the earth, and the sun, and the moon, and the stars, and the mountains, and the trees, and the animals and many of mankind prostrate themselves to Allah? But there are many on whom punishment has become due. And the one whomAllah puts to disgrace, there is none to give him respect. Verily, Allah does what He wills.

(Al-Ḥajj 22:18)

Walking in Redwood National Park among the giant trees is an inexpressible feeling. The park is especially live at dawn when the redwoods release a subtle fragrance with an earthy undertone. As we observe the redwoods, we may feel mes-merized by their height and impressed by their obedience. Recite the *dhikr* of *subhānallahi wabihamdihi* among the red-woods, and one may feel as if the trees are witnessing and participating in the *dhikr* of Allah ﷻ.

Trees, when standing on the ground constitute a simple structure of a wooden trunk and a green leafy canopy, but inside every tree is a world where several hundred systems work simultaneously. For example, the sequoia trees of California have a thick trunk with chemicals that repel insects and make the tree fire-resistant – not fire-proof exactly, but the trees can survive most forest fires. As they grow, the trees add a new ring of wood to their girth every year, and we can determine their age by counting the rings on the trunks. The oldest rings are the smallest and near the center. When it comes to nutrition, have we ever wondered how these giants transport water from the soil all the way to their leaves? It is possible thanks to an extensive system for raising water through the trunk against gravity, and the process of transpiration, whereby leaves "exhale" water vapors. Allah ﷻ taught us the physiological process of osmosis – flow of the water across the membrane – through the trees.

Currently, the largest tree on our planet is a sequoia named General Sherman, about 275 feet in height and tremendously thick, approximately 52,508 cubic feet. The tree is 2200 years old, which means that it was planted even before Isa ﷺ came into this world, *subhānallah*.

Have you not seen how Allah has set forth a parable? A good word is like a good tree, having its root firmly fixed and its branches (reach) to the sky...

(Ibrāhīm 14:24)

How big will the trees be in Jannah? The Prophet ﷺ once said, "In Paradise, there is a tree in whose shade a rider could travel for a hundred years without crossing it" (Tirmidhi 2523).

Allah ﷻ has made the plants and trees such that almost all the living beings on the planet benefit from them. Trees are almost universally a kind of shelter. Fungi, bacteria, and small insects thrive in their roots. Birds make their nests in the canopy and feed on the seedlings. Humans rely on trees for food, timber, and many other necessities. Regardless of their size, trees help everyone in society. For example, the Soaptree yucca at White Sands National Park is like a small marketplace. The plant was once used for making more than one hundred byproducts including soaps, medicines, and fibers for art produced by the Indigenous tribes of the region.

Another park worth mentioning here is Joshua Tree National Park in California, named after the twisted and spiky Joshua trees. They are a distant relative of palm trees and grow only in the Mojave Desert, at a higher altitude. Looking at Joshua trees, recall the beautiful story of a date palm tree that cried for the Prophet ﷺ. Jabir ibn Abdullah narrated that the Prophet ﷺ used to stand by a certain date palm tree when he delivered the Friday sermon. But when a pulpit was built for him and he climbed it, the date palm tree started crying like a child. The Prophet ﷺ descended and embraced the tree, explaining, "It was crying out of longing for what it used to hear" (Bukhārī 3584).

Our Prophet ﷺ used the date palm as an example on another occasion, when he said to his companions: "Amongst the trees, there is a tree, the leaves of which do not fall and is like a Muslim (standing firm). Tell me the name of that tree." The companions thought about the trees of the desert areas. Ibn Umar thought of the date palm tree but felt shy to answer. The others then asked, "Please inform us what is that tree, O Allah's Messenger ﷺ." He ﷺ replied, "It is the date-palm tree." (Bukhārī 62)

Interestingly, some trees that seem harmful are also beneficial to our ecosystem in other ways. The cacti are the worth-mentioning example here. The saguaro cacti of the Saguaro National Park in Arizona can survive in the desert for up to 150 years. In a place so hot and dry that humans and animals cannot bear it for a few hours, saguaro finds no problem living there with minimal water. Their needles protect them from animal attacks, and their exquisite system of water storage and waxy skin preserves the moisture. Their flowers provide nectar to the desert birds. Even though they look terrifying, cacti are not the most dangerous trees. The most dreadful tree, the tree of Zaqqūm, is the one we have not seen yet, and may Allah ﷻ protect us from its sight, *ameen*.

Ibn 'Abbas ﷺ narrated that the Messenger of Allah ﷺ recited this ayah: *Have the taqwā (consciousness or fear) of Allah as is His due, and do not die except as Muslims"* (Aali-Imran 3:102). Then the Messenger of Allah ﷺ said, "If only a drop of al-Zaqqum were to drip into the abode of the world, it would spoil the peoples' livelihood, so what about the person for whom it is his food?" (Tirmidhī 2585). May Allah ﷻ protect us from its sight, *ameen*.

As humans, we naturally love the presence of a flowing river, but we cannot keep our bare limbs in water for more than a few minutes. The enigmatic mangroves and bald cypress trees of Congaree National Park, however, keep their roots submerged for most, if not all, of their lives, *subhānallah*. Their broad bases and the complex root systems enable them to withstand flooding and drought, giving them the title of "champion trees".

While we most often encounter trees with roots, stems, and leaves, there are plants with no such features, yet they beautify our world and are crucial for the ecosystem. This category of plants includes moss. Allah ﷻ has created more than a hundred species of mosses covering the rainforest of Olympic National Park, a temperate rainforest and one of the most beautiful national parks in the country. Mosses do not have any protective coating and can easily dry out. That is why Allah ﷻ provided them with the moist climate of the rainforest. Their moisture becomes the source of water to nearby plants. We can also witness a live example of epiphytes—plants growing on other plants – in the Olympic National Forest.

Then We caused to grow with it gardens, full of delight. It is not in your ability to cause the growth of their trees. Is there any god along with Allah? No, but they are a people who equate (others with Allah).

(Al-Naml 27:60)

The botanical world is profound, with more than 600,000 species of trees on our planet. They remind us to stay firmly grounded, remembering the One who is the Creator of everything. By doing *dhikr* we not only synchronize with the trees on earth but also plant trees in *Jannah* as explained by our Prophet ﷺ: "On the Night of Ascension (*al-Isra wa l-Miraj*) I met Ibrahim ﷺ who said to me: 'O Muhammad, convey my greetings to your *ummah* and tell them that *Jannah* has a vast plain of pure soil and sweet water and the plants grow there by uttering *subhānallah* (Allah is free from imperfection), *alhamdulillah* (praise be to Allah), *la ilaha illa Allah* (there is no god except Allah), and *Allāhu Akbar* (Allah is Greatest)'" (Tirmidhī 3462).

This world and everything in it is created for human beings, and its sole purpose is to keep us connected with our Creator.

A believer lives in this world with a purpose. The power of *dhikr* protects us from negligence and heedlessness and thus keeps us steadfast on the right path.

3

Fall Foliage

And He knows whatever there is in the land and the sea. Not a leaf falls, but He knows it.

(Al-An'ām 6:59)

Allah ﷻ has made the earth so intricate that it continues to astonish the human mind despite all of our scientific advancements. The more we learn about the natural world, the more we admire the majesty and grandeur of the One who created it. During autumn, the trees change the pigmentation of their leaves. To our eyes, it is an exuberant display of the orange, red, and yellow colors, but knowing the botanical details of it further increases the joy.

Every year, the fall foliage is an absolute delight to see at the Shenandoah National Park. The mountains are decorated with a layer of vibrant colors, as if jellybeans were scattered over them. Note how some trees take a bright orange color, and others take a deep crimson hue. It is delightful to see how Allah ﷻ decides the color of the leaves, and sometimes a single tree has multi-colored leaves on it. The falling of the leaves reminds us of a beautiful *hadith* when the Prophet ﷺ was once passing by a tree with dry leaves. He struck it with his stick, and the leaves started falling. The Prophet ﷺ then said: "Indeed, the *dhikr* of *alhumdulillah, la ilaha illa Allah*, and *Allāhu Akbar* cause the sins to fall from a person just as the leaves of this tree" (Tirmidhī 3533).

When visiting the national parks in the fall season, we find people taking photos and films of the best-looking trees. How often do we think about the science behind the color change? Why do leaves change their color, and how does a tree survive an icy winter to wake up again during spring? Allah ﷻ has kept astonishing details within this process.

We know that trees receive their energy from the sun and store it in the form of sugar and other compounds in their bark. During the winter, the trees must protect themselves from cold, and Allah ﷻ has taught them several techniques to withstand the freezing temperatures. As it gets colder, trees take the energy from the leaves and reserve it in a storage system in their trunks. As a result, the green pigment of the leaves, chlorophyll, is broken down. This depigmentation leads to the orange-yellow tinge on the leaves. The bright color repels harmful insects that may harm the tree during the winter. Shedding the leaves also protects a tree from winter storms because once the leaves are discarded, the wind resistance increases, and the stong forces of a windstorm are distributed equally, *subhānallah*. Now think about the evergreen conifers. They have no leaves but rather spines that are covered with thick anti-freeze material to protect them from the cold. They also shed most of their needles and get new ones in the spring.

How do trees know about the approaching winter? Allah has given them a sense of temperature. They can also sense the length of the daytime. Botanical scientists are still trying to solve the mysteries of the seasonal changes in trees. The rising temperatures of the spring stimulate new leaf growth, and trees get ready to bloom again. The season of autumn is also mentioned in a *hadith* when the Prophet used it to explain the number of years before one could enter the Paradise. He used to pray to Allah, "O Allah! Cause me to live needy and cause me to die needy and gather me with the needy on the Day of Resurrection." 'A'ishah asked: "Why, O Messenger of Allah?" He replied: "Indeed the poor will enter Paradise before the rich by forty autumns. Do not turn away the needy even if (you can only share) a piece of date. Love the needy and be near them, for indeed Allah will make you near Him on the Day of Judgement." (Tirmidhī 2352)

Going for a hike in autumn can be a pleasurable experience for our body and mind. The vibrant colors of the leaves and a walk in the crisp yet calm temperature further adds to its beauty. As we explore the scenery of this season, let's increase the spiritual beauty of our hike by reciting *ayat al-kursi* from Surah al-Baqarah to praise Almighty Allah ﷻ, who gave us the chance to experience the beauty of His created world. The Prophet ﷺ once said: "There is a pinnacle of everything, and the pinnacle of the Qur'an is Surah Al-Baqarah. In it there is an *ayah* which is the master of all *ayaat* in the Qur'an. It is *ayat al-kursi*." (Tirmidhi 2878)

Allah: There is no god but He, the Living, the All- Sustaining. Neither slumber nor sleep overtake Him. To Him belongs whatever is in the heavens and whatever is on the earth. Who can intercede with Him without His permission? He knows what is before them (his creatures) and what is behind them, while they encompass nothing of His knowledge except what He wills. His kursi (chair) extends over the heavens and the earth, and He feels no fatigue in guarding and preserving them. He is the Most High, the Supreme.

(Al-Baqarah 2:255)

4

The Mountains

Say, "Travel in the land and look how He (Allah) has
originated the creation. And then Allah will create the

> *subsequent creation of the Hereafter. Verily, Allah is*
> *powerful to do everything."*
>
> *(Al-'Ankabūt 29:20)*

When we sit in airplanes and look out the window, our imaginations are often captured by two structures in particular: the clouds and the mountains. The giant rocks on the surface of the earth are sometimes brown or red, like in Arizona, or lush green, like in Montana. Allah ﷻ created these mountains so beautifully that we would never get tired of their breathtaking views, whether the Alps of the North Cascades in Washington or the canyons of the Gunnison in Colorado.

As for the earth, We have stretched it out and placed on it firm mountains, and We have caused to grow in it everything well-balanced.

(Al-Ḥijr 15:19)

We have learned from geology that the mountains are formed from the collision of tectonic plates and volcanic activities. They play an important role in stabilizing the surface of the earth. The mountains as we know them have existed on our planet for a very long time. They embody majesty and mystique, seeming to stand still, bearing witness to the changes around them over the millennia.

Did We not make the earth as a bed, and the mountains as pegs?

(Al-Naba 78:6-7)

Like the other creations of Allah ﷻ, mountains are assigned a critical role in the ecosystem. They comprise one fourth of the earth's surface. Some of the world's major freshwater rivers begin their journey in the mountains, and about twenty percent of the electricity we use comes from the hydropower generated from these rivers. Mountains are also the hubs of biodiversity, supporting a large variety of plants and animals, tiny invertebrates, and even microbes.

And We created mountains on the earth, lest it should shake with them, and We have made therein paths and ways, so that they are guided.

(Al-Anbiyā' 21:31)

From the tall mountains to the deep canyons, the spectacular landscapes of mountain ranges speak about the divine glory of Allah ﷻ. All we need to do is to observe it with our *imān,* and we will appreciate that everything in nature is involved in the *dhikr* of Allah ﷻ.

Our hikes should not be limited to just observation or exercise. Rather, the whole experience can become a process of spiritual cleansing. When going on a steep hike, we can make the entire experience memorable by playing the recitation of the Qur'an on our phone – especially Surah Al-Yasin. When passing through a forest, we might feel the resonance of the *dhikr* of Allah more deeply.

All the seven skies and the earth and all those therein extol His glory. And there is not a single thing that does not extol His glory, but you do not understand their extolling. Surely, He is Forbearing, Most-Forgiving.

(Banī Isrā'īl 17: 44)

In the state of Colorado, we have the majestic Rockies of the Rocky Mountain National Park, favorites for many of us, known for their captivating beauty. These world-famous mountains are also known for their gemstones, including amethyst, aquamarine, smoky quartz, agate, and even diamonds. Imagine a mountain made from gemstones and gold – how much can one profit from it? And that is what Allah ﷻ offered to our Prophet ﷺ. When the Quraysh asked the Prophet ﷺ to turn the mount of Safa into gold, the angel Jibraeel ﷺ came to the Prophet ﷺ and asked if he ﷺ would like the valley to be turned into gold or, instead, the door of mercy. Our beloved Prophet ﷺ chose the *akhirah* in the form of repentance and mercy instead of the temporary gains of this world (Ahmad 2167). *SubhānAllah.*

Now let's reflect upon our own choices. What have we chosen in this world? Are we collecting gold? Or are we thinking about our savings for the *akhirah*?

When the earth will be jolted with a terrible jolt, and the mountains will be crumbled until they become dust, scattered in the air…

(Al-Wāqi'ah 56:4-5)

Mountains are essentially giant rocks planted firmly in the ground, yet they are shaped and carved in a way that each is unique from the next mountain on the same foothill. Within the Appalachian Mountains in the southeastern part of the country are the Great Smoky mountains and the Great Smoky Mountains National Park.

Mashā'Allāh we say when we witness the Great Smoky Mountains, especially during autumn when they are covered by the fog that inspired their name. When observing the Smoky Mountains, we can bring to mind the *hadith* when our beloved Prophet 🌸 looked at Mount Uhud and gave an important teaching about voluntary charity (*sadaqah*), saying that if he had a mountain of gold equal to the mountain of Uhud, he would make sure to give it all away except for what little he might need to repay debts (Bukhārī 6444). Such was the level of generosity of our Prophet 🌸.

The remote and rugged wilderness of Guadalupe Mountains National Park is another favorite of many travelers. The Guadalupe Mountains were once covered in the ocean, but now they stand tall above sea level and wear a thick blanket of minerals and a unique marine fossil reef. They provide homes to the plants and animals of the Chihuahuan desert, including prickly pear cacti, yuccas, and agave trees, along with snakes, coyotes, and lizards. Whether in bone-chilling cold or scorching heat, the animals and plants continue to receive their provision (*rizq*) from Allah ﷻ.

Mountains have always been features of our planet. Imagine people five thousand years ago, looking at the same mountain and enjoying the view. Where have all those people gone, and what are they doing right now? They have departed from this temporary world. Death is the ultimate reality of this life. One day, we shall be gone, too.

Once a companion from the Ansar came to the Prophet ﷺ and asked which of the believers are the best. The Prophet ﷺ replied, "Those with the best manners." The companion then asked which of the believers are the wisest, and the Prophet ﷺ said, "Those who remember their death and prepare for it" (Ibn Mājah 4259).

A day will come when the mountains too will experience death. As mentioned in the Qur'an:

And when the sky will be split, and when the mountains will be blown away as dust...

(Al-Mursalāt 77:9-10)

There was one mountain, however, that collapsed into dust several thousand years ago, during the time of the Prophet Musa ﷺ.

When Musa came at Our appointed time and his Lord spoke to him, he said, "My Lord, show (Yourself) to me that I may look upon You." He (Allah) said: "You cannot see Me. But look upon the mountain. If it stays at its place, you shall see Me." So when his Lord appeared to the mountain, He made it collapse to dust, and Musa fell down unconscious. When he recovered, he said: "Glory be to You. I turn to You in repentance, and I am the first of the believers."

(Al-A'rāf 7:143)

The Rio Grande River sets the boundary between the United States and Mexico. Here we have the Chisos Mountains of the

Big Bend National Park, known for their extreme wilderness and blazing summer heat.

Home to some of the most exceptional desert landscapes, Big Bend is a test of our hiking abilities. Let's recite the *dhikr* of Allah as we climb up the mountain:

سُبْحَانَ اللَّهِ وَبِحَمْدِهِ سُبْحَانَ اللَّهِ الْعَظِيمِ

Glory be to Allah, and all praise is due to Him. Glory be to Allah the Greatest.

Abu Huraira reported that Allah's Messenger ﷺ said: "Two phrases which are light on the tongue but heavy on the scale and dear to the Compassionate One are *subhanallahi wabihamdihi, subhanallahi l-adheem*." (Sahih Muslim 2694)

When walking up on one of the mountains, remember the times when the Prophet ﷺ used to climb Jabal al-Noor ("the Mountain of Light") in Makkah to find solitude so he could submerge himself in the *dhikr*. Remembering Allah ﷻ and meditating was a part of his life even before the prophethood. And then the time came when the first revelation was sent by Allah ﷻ through Jibraeel ﷺ:

Recite with the name of your Lord who created (everything), He created man from a clot of blood. Read, and your Lord is the most gracious, who imparted knowledge by means of the pen. He taught man what he did not know.

(Al- 'Ālāq 96:1-5)

Are these mountains always going to stand here, tall and strong? Allah ﷻ reminds us in the Qur'an to observe the massive structure of the mountains. This is to remind us of the time when these huge rocks would be nothing but sand. Today they are standing high on the surface of the earth. On the Day of Resurrection, they will scatter like dust.

They ask you about the mountains. So, say (to them), "My Lord will crush them into particles of dust, then will turn them into a leveled plain in which you will see neither a curve nor an uneven place."

(ТаНа 20:105-107)

Then, once the trumpet will be blown for the first time, and the earth and the mountains will be lifted and crushed into pieces with a single blow...

(Al-Ḥāqqah 69:13-14)

There are many other mountain ranges on our planet. Whether the Himalayas or the Alps, the sublime structure of the mountains conveys a similar message to their visitors: how minuscule a human is, and how short the time we have on this planet. There were people who climbed these mountains before us, and there will be many who come after us to undertake similar expeditions. What we take with us from this world is really all that matters.

Therefore, when hiking through the mountains we must remember the time that is sure to come. Are we ready for the judgment of our deeds? Have we established any ongoing charities (*sadaqah jariya*) that will benefit us when we are gone?

(It is a) a day when people will be like scattered moths, and the mountains will be like carded wool.

(Al-Qāri'ah 101:4-5)

On the day when the earth and the mountains will violently
shake, and the mountains will be a heap of sand poured out...
(Al-Muzzammil 73:14)

One might have a practical question about what type of *dhikr* is best when exploring the mountains. The answer is simple. Allah's *dhikr* can have various forms. It is not limited to the recitation of the Qur'an and praising and glorifying the Almighty with specific Arabic supplications. It also includes making *du'ā'* in our own words and being grateful for our many blessings, like saying *alhamdulillah* for the body that is physically fit and able to travel. Anything that brings our mind closer to the remembrance of Allah ﷻ is *dhikr*. Even praising Allah's creation – in this case, nature itself, the giant mountains, and the small plants and their details – is part of His remembrance. Because mountain hikes can become strenuous at times and the recitation of the Qur'an and detailed supplications may be difficult to maintain, some scholars have suggested reciting *tasbih* when trekking at high elevations. One well-known example would be the tasbih of Fatima, from the sunnah of our Prophet: *subhanallah, alhamdulillah,*

Allāhu Akbar. This particular *dhikr* delivers an instant boost of physical energy and spiritual happiness.

Let's continue our journey and reflect on more features of our natural world.

5

Vastness of a desert

And those who disbelieve, their deeds are like a mirage in a desert. The thirsty one thinks it to be water, until he comes up to it, and he finds it to be nothing, but he finds Allah

with him, Who will pay him his due (Hell). And Allah is Swift at reckoning.

(Al-Nūr 24:39)

Sandy deserts are usually found in hotter climates, far from civilization. However, there is a desert in California that lies between the San Juan and the Sangre de Cristo mountain ranges, just a short distance from urban city life. The Great Sand Dunes National Park is where the sand dunes may go up to 750 feet tall. The desert at an elevation of 7000 feet may seem strange to the human mind, like an illusion, but it displays the greatness of Allah ﷻ, Who is capable of creating anything, anywhere He wants. Great Sand Dunes National Park is known for its silence, as the sand absorbs the noise. Because of its higher altitude, the sand is free of venomous creatures such as snakes and scorpions. The desert is cooler during the winter but scorching hot in the summer, up to 150 degrees Fahrenheit! Looking at the hot sand of the desert, one may recollect the story of Bilal Ibn Rabah, our Prophet's beloved companion. Bilal ؓ was laid on the hot sand of the Arabian desert. His vicious enslaver, Umayya ibn Khalaf, put heavy stones on Bilal's chest to force him to renounce the *deen*. Bilal was told to call upon the idols that the pagan Arabs worshipped, but instead, Bilal ﷺ repeated *Ahad, Ahad*, Allah is one. His patience in withstanding Umayya's cruelty was witnessed by Abu Bakr al-Siddiq ﷺ, who convinced Umayya to sell Bilal to him so he could set him free. By the power of his *imān* and his love for the Prophet ﷺ, Bilal's rank reached so high that his footsteps were heard in Jannah.

Abu Hurairah ﷺ narrated that the Prophet ﷺ once asked Bilal at the time of *fajr*, "Tell me of the best deed you did after embracing Islam, for I heard your footsteps in front of me in Paradise." Bilal ﷺ replied, "I did not do anything worth mentioning except that whenever I performed ablution during the day or night, I prayed after it as much as was written for me." (Bukhārī 1149)

As we continue through the deserts, we come to an unusual place in the state of New Mexico. While deserts usually consist of brown or clay-colored sand, there is one that is as white as milk and shiny as crystal. Allah ﷻ has placed the largest gypsum sand dunes in White Sands National Park. Walking on white sand of this desert feels like being on a different planet. The sandy expanse occupies an area of more than two hundred square miles. The deep layers of gypsum and sand are held together by water that lies underneath. The sand of White Sands National Park is soft as a carpet and remains cool throughout the year, even during the summer. The scene – a white desert with bluish-gray mountains on the horizon – could not have been imagined by a human mind, *subhānallah*.

To the west we find another geological wonder that astonishes the human mind, the Death Valley National Park. It is a strange place, encompassing more than 3.5 million acres, less than one percent of which is sand. Death Valley has diverse geologic features, including more than 50 types of rock formations and distinctly colored mountains, each made from a different type of elemental rock: purple comes from manganese, green from mica, and red from oxidized rock, to name a few, *subhānallah*.

The park is 282 feet below sea level and is one of the hottest and driest places on our planet. The desert of Death Valley might remind us of the Battle of Tabūk when many soldiers avoided joining the Prophet ﷺ due to extreme heat. The Prophet ﷺ gathered an army of 30,000 men and marched towards the valley of Tabūk. When their water supplies finished and thirst became unbearable, Allah ﷻ provided water with a downpour of rain upon the desert. Such was the level of imān of our ancestors who fought in the path of Allah ﷻ in some of the most extreme situations. Those who used weather as an excuse, Allah ﷻ replied to them in Surah Tawbah:

Those who stayed away (from the expedition of Tabūk) rejoiced at remaining behind and not accompanying the Messenger of Allah. They hated to strive in the Cause of Allah with their belonging and their lives and told others: "Do not go forth in this fierce heat." Tell them: "The fire of Hell is more intense in heat."

(Al-Tawbah 9:81)

Death Valley National Park also contains the largest protected salt flats in the world. It is an enclosed basin covered with salt that is too harsh for plants and animals to survive. Looking at the barren land, imagine the uncultivated valley where Hajar had to walk with her baby Ismail ﷺ, and there was no shade or water nearby. She ran seven times between the mountains of Safa and Marwa with the hope that Allah ﷻ would send help. Allah ﷻ answered the prayer of the mother, and water started pouring from the ground. Today we drink that special water of Zam Zam from the same well. Zam Zam is colorless and odorless but has a distinctive sweet taste like no other water on earth. *Subhānallah.*

Death Valley National Park is too hot to visit during the summer. The temperature is usually above 122 degrees Fahrenheit. Imagine standing barefoot in front of Allah on the day when the sun will be so close that people will be drowning in their sweat. Such will be the heat on the day of *Qiyāmah,* the Day of Resurrection. Only those under the shade of His throne will be protected from the heat, as explained by the Prophet ﷺ. "Seven (people) will be shaded by Allah on the Day of Resurrection when there will be no shade except His shade: a just ruler, a young man who has been brought up in the worship of Allah, a man who remembers Allah in seclusion and his eyes are then flooded with tears, a man whose heart is attached to mosques (offering his compulsory congregational prayers in the mosque), two men who love each other for Allah's sake, a man who is called by a charming lady of noble birth to commit illegal sexual intercourse and he says, 'I am afraid of Allah,' and a man who gives in charity so secretly that his left hand does not know what his right hand has given" (Bukhārī 6806).

There are more deserts in America, and many more on our planet, but the message of the desert is the same, to remember the spiritual connection with the One who created all kinds of landscapes for us.

6

Valleys and Canyons

And We created mountains on the earth, lest it should shake with them, and We have made therein broad highways for them to pass through, so that they are guided.

(Al-Anbiyā' 21:31)

The above *āyah* references the concept of a canyon, and among the national parks in the U.S., the Grand Canyon may be the best example. According to geologists, a canyon is formed by a process called downcutting. As the river cuts down into the earth, it erodes the rocks. Water, being an entity with no shape or weight, when given power by Allah ﷻ, erodes rocks, carves mountains, and flows through them as rivers. Every year, millions of visitors come to see Grand Canyon National Park from all over the world. People benefit from the stories of the Indigenous tribes and take pictures near the gorge. Amidst a number of other materialistic distractions stands the giant canyon with the Colorado River flowing through it, testifying to Allah's magnificent geological miracles. There is another canyon like the Grand Canyon, but it seems to have been formed without water: the Valles Marineris Canyon on the planet Mars, thought to be the largest canyon in our solar system. There are likely many other wonders in the solar system unknown to mankind. *Subhānallah.*

The deep calmness of the Grand Canyon dampens the sound of the visiting crowds, and as we hike down, we hear the winds whistling as if the mountains are busy in the *dhikr* of Allah ﷻ. If we listen closely, the mountains might tell us that no bucket list can bring peace and serenity to the heart other than the *dhikr* of the *Rahmān* and *Raheem*. We can admire the canyons and take their photos, but joining them in doing the *dhikr* of Allah is an experience like no other on this planet.

Or the One who made the earth a place to settle and made rivers amidst it and made mountains for (making) it (firm), and made a barrier between two seas? Is there any god along with Allah? No, but most of them do not have knowledge.
(Al-Naml 27:61)

In Utah we find the world-famous Zion National Park, home of iconic rock formations. Zion is often on the bucket list of nature photographers and travel enthusiasts. The hiking trails are dangerous, some only for experienced hikers. While some people climb these tracks for peak-bagging and selfies, we can keep in mind Prophet Mūsa ﷺ and the steep slope of Mount Toor, which he climbed to speak with the Creator of this universe, Allah ﷻ. What a blessing it was to sit and talk to the One who controls all living beings. But how did these conversations begin? It is explained beautifully by Allah ﷻ in Surah TāHā:

Has there come to you the story of Musa? He saw a fire and said to his family, "Stay here. I have noticed a fire. Perhaps I can bring you an ember from it, or find some guidance by the fire." So, when he came to it, he was called, "O Musa, it is Me, your Lord, so remove your shoes; you are in the sacred valley of Tuwa. I have chosen you (for prophethood), so listen to what is revealed: Verily, I am Allah. There is no god but Me, so worship Me, and perform salah for My remembrance."

(TāHā 20:9-14)

While Zion National Park is popular for its steep hikes and entrenched rivers, its neighbor, Bryce Canyon National Park, is known for its untouched poetic beauty and serene vistas capped by snow. According to the experts, the canyons were once underwater, which explains the sedimentation of minerals. Tectonic plate activity raised the Colorado Plateau, and as the water evaporated, the canyons rose to the surface of the earth. *Subhānallah.*

Have not those who disbelieve known that heavens and the earth were joined together as one united piece, then We parted them? And We created from water every living thing. Will they not then believe?

(Al-Anbiyā' 21:30)

Apart from their beauty, the canyons are known for their unique geological details. Bryce Canyon National Park contains thehighest concentration of limestone hoodoos, the bulbous statues of rock made from constant weathering and erosion over time. Unlike other places where flowing water carves the canyon, here the rocks get their shape from the snow. Bryce Canyon has a cycle of warm days and freezing nights, and as the snow melts, water percolates inside the fractured rocks. At night when the water refreezes, the rock expands and cracks. This cycle of weathering and erosion never stops, and the dynamic cliffs continue to impress visitors with their astonishing look.

Humans also undergo the process of weathering and erosion through their mistakes and sins. Repair can be done through constant repentance and following the sunnah of our beloved

Prophet ﷺ. As we observe the fascinating rocks of Bryce Canyon, we can return our mind to the remembrance of Allah ﷻ, the master planner of this geological paragon in the desert of Utah.

As for the earth, We have spread it out, and set therein mountains standing firm, and caused to grow therein every kind of delightful growth (plants).

(Qaf 50:7)

Another area to observe the enchanted rocks is in the wild and rugged Canyonlands National Park, a place where Allah ﷻ has displayed striking ecological diversity for us. From the mountaintops with minimal water to the grassy meadows in the valley, the national park showcases various environmental regions in one place. One area of the park gets less than ten inches of rain but provides a home to pinyon-juniper trees that are capable of surviving in harsh climates. The other area contains a river with abundant wildlife around it, including deer, bobcats, and beavers. The hiking trails at the Canyonlands are known for their rapid descents, some up to a thousand feet, and excellent views of the sandstone cliffs. There are canyons within canyons as far as the eye can see. Let's not forget to say *subhānallah* as we hike down and *Allāhu Akbar* as we go uphill. Jabir ibn Abdullah narrates that the Prophet ﷺ used to say *Allāhu Akbar* when walking uphill and *subhānallah* when walking downhill (Bukhārī 2993).

Hiking in nature also provides an excellent opportunity to recall the active lifestyle of our Prophet ﷺ. He ﷺ used to hike the mountains of Makkah and Medina, modeling for us the importance of staying physically fit.

Abu Hurairah ﷺ narrated that he did not see anyone walking faster than the Prophet ﷺ. The companions used to find it difficult to keep pace when walking with him, and he was just walking at his normal pace (Tirmidhi).

To the west, we find a spectacular ancient volcano in the Salina Valley of California, in the less well-known Pinnacles National Park. Like the bigger mountains, the pinnacles also have their geological origin in tectonic plate activity and volcanic fields. On our hike, we will notice the spires and crags that are home to California condors, one of the largest birds in the world. Condors can have a wingspan of 9.5 feet and fly with a speed of 55 miles per hour, and more than 150 miles per day, at 15 thousand feet altitude. Thinking of birds in this valley, we can recall the story of Prophet Ibrahim ﷺ:

And (remember) when Ibrahim said, "My Lord, show me how You give life to the dead." He said: "Do you do not believe?" He said: "Yes (I believe), but it is to be stronger in faith." He said: "Then take four birds and tame them to your call, then (slaughter them and cut them into pieces and) put a portion of them on every hill, then call them, and they shall come to you rushing. And know that Allah is Mighty and Wise."

(Al-Baqarah 2:260)

Traveling through nature while admiring the creation of Allah ﷻ refreshes our *imān* in a way that no ordinary travel can. Let's continue our journey and visit areas known for their extensive cave systems.

His purity is proclaimed by all that is in the heavens and the earth, and He is the All-Mighty, the All-Wise.

(Al-Hashr 59:24)

7

The Caves

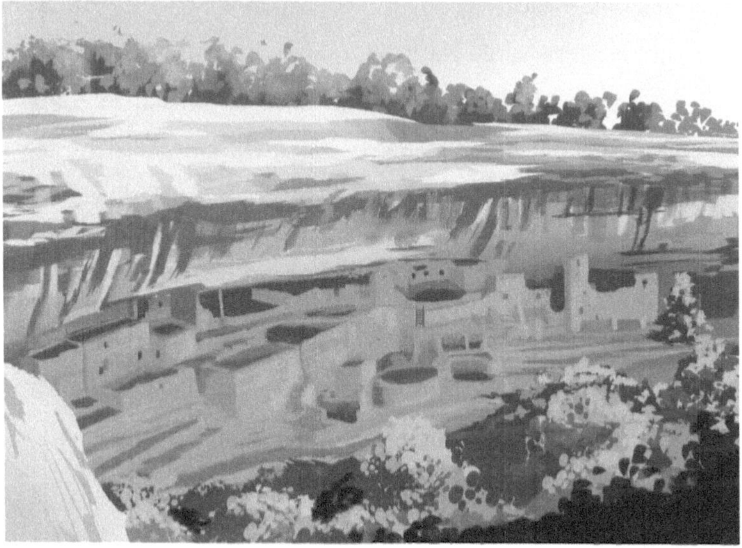

And you carve houses from the hills with pride.

(Al-Shu'arā' 26:149)

Not all national parks have mountains, and not all mountains have animals or trees upon them. There is a national park in Colorado that gives us a glimpse of an ancient civilization, a bustling town where humans once lived. We are at the Mesa Verde National Park. According to historians, it was home to the ancient Pueblo people several thousand years ago, long before the continent was colonized by the Europeans. The dwellings, however, look as if they were built in the recent past.

Many patterns of behavior (and mishaps) have passed before you. So, traverse the land and see what the end of those was who disbelieved (in the Oneness of Allah) and disobeyed (the prophets).

(Āali-'Imrān 3:137)

The ruins of the cliff dwellings were encountered by the Europeans in the 1700s. We imagine they were carved by humans before any powerful machinery existed. According to archeologists, the people of the dwellings seem to have disappeared almost overnight, never to be found again. Only Allah ﷻ knows the truth.

Have they not traveled through and seen what was the end of those before them? Most of them were greater in number than these and mightier in strength, and in the traces (they have left behind them) in the land; yet all that they used to earn did not work for them at all.

(Al-Mu'min 40:82)

The ancient ruins of Mesa Verde National Park remind us of the story of Prophet Saleh ﷺ, who was sent to the polytheistic people of al-Hijr, the clan of Thamud. They were known for their architectural skill in carving homes into the mountains. Today, the remains of their mountain homes still exist in Yemen, displaying the supreme power of Allah ﷻ Who crushed the pride and arrogance of the transgressors. When the Prophet Mohammad ﷺ passed through the habitations of al-Hijr he instructed his companions to pass quickly through the valley and to not drink water from the well, to protect them from the calamity that fell upon the people of al-Hijr (Muslim 2980b).

Our journey through the national parks gives us not only mountain views but also education about what lies inside these gigantic structures. *Subhānallah*, how amazing is Allah 🌸 who created a diverse ecosystem on the surface of the giant rocks as well as a completely different world inside them, in the form of caves. People often do not think about exploring the underground structures. Perhaps this is the reason why Mammoth Cave and Carlsbad Caverns National Parks are not as popular amongst the visitors.

Believed to be one of the largest cave systems on our planet, Mammoth Cave National Park is home to several thousand years of human history. Geologically, the caves were formed when the mixture of rainwater and soil turned into a weak acid. Over time, this acidic water squeezed through the rocks and grew channels, finally resulting in a cave. The continuous passage of water makes a way through hard rock that otherwise would have seemed impossible to penetrate, *subhānallah*. We can relate this continuous behavior to our good deeds. Small continuous good deeds, like praying extra *nafl* or a having a designated time for *dhikr* on a daily basis, are so beloved to Allah 🌸 that they *insha'Allah* will ease our path to Jannah like water makes a path through rock.

As we walk through the cave entrance, imagine the time over 1400 years ago when the Prophet ﷺ and Abu Bakr ؓ took refuge from assassins in the Cave of Thawr. A spider covered the entrance to make it look unoccupied. Abu Bakr ؓ was worried about his best friend's safety – and what an amazing best friend Abu Bakr ؓ had – but our Prophet ﷺ was calm because of his *taqwā* (consciousness of Allah) and his strong faith and reliance only on Allah ﷻ. The story is a beautiful reminder that no harm can reach us if it is against the will of Allah ﷻ, and whatever the situation is, we must have complete trust in Allah's decree.

When you have turned away from them and those whom they worship other than Allah, then seek refuge in the cave, and your Lord will open a way for you from His mercy and provide you with ease in your matters.

(Al-Kahf 18:16)

Rerouting back to the national parks, the caves of Carlsbad Caverns National Park originated from a reef in an inland sea.

As the reef rose above the water, the sponge work cavities in the cave were filled with hydrogen sulfide gas, which later oxidized into sulfur. Bacteria converted sulfur into sulfuric acid, which finally caused the conversion of limestone to gypsum, the main mineral in the cave.

He (Musa) said, "Our Lord is the one who gave everything its due shape, then guided it aright."
(TaHa 20:50)

Walking inside "the big room" of Carlsbad Caverns is like walking into someone else's drawing room, where an entirely different language is spoken. The minerals in the cave form the structures called stalactites and stalagmites. Stalactites are the projections from the cave ceiling, whereas stalagmites grow from the cave floor. Rainwater drips pass through the limestone bed and absorbs carbon dioxide from the air, turning it into carbonic acid crystals for our display. However much our own technologies have advanced, the mysterious caves of Carlsbad continue to amaze their visitors. What a magnificent planet Allah Almighty created for us. Everything in nature has a universe of knowledge inside it.

Do you think that the People of the Cave and the inscription (the news or the name of the people of the cave) were, from Our signs, a wonder?

(Al-Kahf 18:9)

As we walk into the cave, Let's reflect on the surah in the Qur'an where Allah talks about the famous People of the Cave:

And you might have seen the sun, when it rose, declining to the right from their cave; and when it set, it bypassed them towards the left, while they lay in the midst of the cave. That is one of the signs of Allah. Whomsoever Allah guides is rightly guided, and whomsoever He sends astray, for him you will find no one to protect, no one to lead (to the right path).

(Al-Kahf 18:17)

Surah al-Kahf is also important because the Prophet ﷺ used to recite it every Friday and, according to Abu Darda ؓ, asked us to learn the first ten verses of Surah al-Kahf for protection against the False Messiah (Muslim 809a).

They stayed in their cave for three hundred years (solar years) and added nine (lunar years).

(Al-Kahf 18:25)

When we visit Mammoth Cave National Park, the park rangers provide a guided tour of the cave to visitors. Once a group is inside the cave, the ranger turns off the lights for a few seconds. The cave becomes terrifyingly dark, so much so that opening or closing one's eyes make no difference. This experience of a few seconds provides us a chance to imagine our grave, the darkness and solitude of it. May Allah 🌸 protect us from the punishment of the grave, *ameen*.

Once the Prophet 🌸 asked his companions about an elderly woman who used to clean the mosque. On hearing that she had passed away, the Prophet 🌸 went to see her grave and said, "Verily, these graves are full of darkness for their dwellers. Allah the Almighty illuminates them for their occupants by my prayer over them." (Muslim 956)

May Allah 🌸 make our graves spacious and illuminate them for us, *ameen*.

8

The Landscape

*And We placed towering mountains therein and provided
you with sweet water to drink.*

(Al-Mursalāt 77:27)

When people think of a beautiful landscape, they often imagine a place with mountains, deep canyons, and a wide blue sky. A topographic landscape usually has the basic ingredients such as tall mountains, lush green trees, and a body of water, a river, or a lake. However, it is fascinating to see how different the landscapes on our planet look despite having similar basic elements. Whether it is the scenery of Denali National Park in Alaska or Acadia National Park of Maine, the topography of each national park is unique. *Subhānallah.*

As for the earth, We have spread it out, and cast on it firm hills, and caused to grow therein every kind of delightful thing, as a source of vision and as a lesson to every servant (of Allah) who turns (to Him for guidance).

(Qāf 50:7-8)

Allah ﷻ has beautified this world for us. He made us capable of exploring it so we can observe nature and remember His magnificence. One such place that showcases the exquisite rhythms of nature is Yosemite National Park of California. It is the most visited national park in the world and continues to be on the wish list of many. The valley is known for its year-round natural activities. The landscape of Yosemite, carved originally by glaciers, is enriched with fruitful meadows for its wildlife.

He is the One who sent down water from the heavens, of which you have your drink; and with it (you grow) plants on which you pasture your cattle.

(Al-Naḥl 16:10)

Many visitors to Yosemite Valley remark on the mighty waterfalls and the Merced River. A believer can however use the same scenery to praise the Omnipotence of Allah ﷻ. Look at the massive granite cliffs displaying one of the largest waterfalls in the world, Yosemite Falls, about 4425 feet in height. *Subhānallah.*

How well We poured water, and how nicely We split the earth in clefts, then We grew in it grain and grapes and clover plants (i.e., green fodder for the cattle).

('Abasa 80:25-27)

The non-stop waterfalls of Yosemite flow into the Merced River, and from there the water is supplied to brooks and streams. Who else can run the world with such perfection, other than Allah 🕮? Water, a necessity of life, is distributed through a system that begins with the snow covering the mountains, flowing down in cascades and rivers, finally reaching everyone to fulfill their needs. In fact, our bodies are made from sixty percent water, and we need it for all of our essential functions, including temperature regulation.

And He is the One who sends the winds as heralds of glad tidings, going before his Mercy (rain); and We sent down purifying water from the sky, so that We revive a dead land therewith, and We give drink to the many cattle and humans created by Us.

(Al-Furqān 25:48-49)

Many humans and animals can survive without food for a few weeks, but we cannot survive without water for more than three days. That is why providing water to the thirsty is one of the best *sadaqah jariyah* that continues to add good deeds to our account even after death. Satisfying someone's thirst brings the mercy of Allah and pleases Him. Abu Huraira 🕮 narrated from the Prophet 🕮 a story of a man who went to a well to drink water. As he drank water, he saw a dog panting with thirst. He felt for the dog and went down the well and filled his shoe with water. He then gave the water to the dog, alleviating his suffering. Allah forgave this man because of his good deed. People who were listening to this story asked the Prophet 🕮 if there is a reward for serving animals. The Prophet 🕮 replied, "Yes there is a reward for serving any living being" (Bukhārī 2363).

What would happen to the world if all the water evaporated? Who would be able to bring the water back, other than the Lord who created it?

Say, "Tell me, should your water vanish into the earth, who then can supply you with flowing water?
(Al-Mulk 67:30)

Moving on, let's talk about the vastness of the Pacific Ocean, our planet's largest and deepest ocean. The beaches of the Pacific Ocean are beautiful everywhere, but the ones in

California are known for their exquisite beauty. However, many people in the state, particularly in the city of Los Angeles, are often so busy with their lives that they are unaware of unincorporated islands full of nature's bounties less than two hours away from them. The Channel Islands National Park is isolated but not unreachable. A year-round ferry can take us to the three islands, and the ride on the Pacific Ocean is even more spectacular than the islands themselves.

Did you not see that ships sail through the sea by the grace of Allah, so He may show you some of His signs? Verily, there are signs for every man of patience and gratitude.
(Luqmān 31:31)

The ocean is a different world in itself. From the kelp forests and algae to the gigantic whales and crustaceans, creatures great and small, all have their peaceful space. As we move against the strong tides of the Pacific Ocean, we might catch a glimpse of whales and dolphins. A whale can remind us of the story of Yunus ﷺ, who was swallowed by a whale. While inside the body of the largest mammal on earth, he remembered Allah ﷻ in one of the most beautiful ways:

Then the fish swallowed him when he was reproaching his own self. Had he not been of those who proclaim Allah's glory, he would have definitely lived in its belly till the day when the dead will be raised.

(Al- Ṣāffāt 37:142-144)

The supplication made by Yunus ﷺ is mentioned in Surah al-Anbiya and is commonly known as *ayat al-karima*.

"There is no god but You. Glory be to You. Indeed I was among the wrongdoers."

(Al-Anbiyā'21:87)

When looking at the water we get a hint of the vastness of the ocean and the sheer amount of water on our planet. The water is also doing the *dhikr* of Allah ﷻ. Its *dhikr* can be seen in its strict obedience to its boundaries, even though the waves of an ocean are strong enough to tear down any man-made structure. The water also obeyed Allah ﷻ when it had to make a way for Musa ﷺ, *subhānallah*:

Then we revealed to Musa, "Strike the sea with your staff." So it was severed apart, and each part became like a big mountain.

(Al-Shu'arā' 26:63)

On our scenic expedition, we might visit several other perfect landscapes, like Denali National Park in Alaska with its pristine wilderness, and Acadia National Park in Maine, where thick coniferous forests accommodate several hundred species of birds. Allah ﷻ has not only blessed us with natural wonders all around us but has also enlightened our mind with scientific knowledge about His creations. Today we have the machinery to construct smooth roads through mountains. As a result, we are able to enjoy scenic drives like the one through Grand Teton National Park in Wyoming or the Million Dollar Highway in Colorado.

To the East of the United States, we have The New River Gorge in the Appalachian mountains. Unlike its name, The gorge was made by one of the oldest rivers in the world and is now a part of New River Gorge National Park in West Virginia. Allah ﷻ carved through the rocky Appalachian plateaus with the ever-flowing whitewater river, providing water to millions of trees nearby. Humans also take advantage of the river for fishing and recreation like whitewater rafting.

One may wonder, of all the remarkable national parks, which one is the most beautiful. While each of them is given special characteristics by Allah ﷻ, there is one amongst them made so beautifully in its landscape that people momentarily forget their problems and difficulties when they experience its breathtaking scenery. People may have different opinions on this, but I personally consider Glacier National Park in Montana to be the most scenic of all the national parks.

(He is) the One who made the earth a bed (spread out) for you, and made in it pathways for you to move, and sent down water (rain) from the sky; and We brought forth various kinds of vegetations...

(ṬāHā 20:53)

At the first sight of Glacier National Park, it feels as if a part of Paradise has come down to earth. Commonly known as the "Crown of the Continent", Glacier National Park is often cited as one of the most beautiful places in North America. The main body of water, Lake McDonald, is blessed with crystal-clear water and colorful rocks. The panoramic reflection of the surrounding mountains on the lake further adds to the beauty. As we go up the mountain, we get to enjoy lush green valleys, waterfalls, wildflowers, and glaciers, all under the great sky over Montana. Wherever we look, on every head turn, there is a different scene made of the same basic elements of mountain, lake, and trees, but this is what makes Glacier National Park so unique. *Subhānallah.*

Say, "Praise belongs to Allah, and peace be on those of His servants whom He has chosen." Is it not He Who created the heavens and earth and sent down for you water (rain) from the sky? Then We caused to grow with it gardens, full of delight. It is not in your ability to cause the growth of their trees. Is there any god along with Allah? No, but they are a people who equate (others with Allah).

(Al-Naml 27:59-60)

Whether it is Glacier National Park or any other landscape, they all represent the natural beauty of this temporary world.

As we explore the picturesque meadows, we must not forget to think about the unimaginable beauty of Jannah, as explained by the Prophet ﷺ who told us that Allah said, "I have prepared such excellent things for My righteous slaves that no eye has ever seen, nor an ear heard, nor a human heart can ever think of" (Bukhārī 7498).

This temporary life will end soon, but for the ones who believe in *laa ilaha illa Allah,* there is an eternal life promised in Jannah. Allah has described *Jannah* in many verses in the Qur'an.

Allah has promised the believers, men and women, gardens beneath which rivers flow to dwell therein forever, and beautiful mansions in the gardens of eternity. And Allah's pleasure is above all. That is the supreme success.

(Al-Tawbah 9:72)

As we explore the beauty of Glacier National Park,we must not forget that the Prophet ﷺ once mentioned that "the smallest of space in Jannah (as small as occupied by a whip) is better than everything in this world" (Bukhārī 6415).

The Prophet 🌸 once walked through the market and noticed a dead lamb with very short ears. He 🌸 asked his companions if they would like to get this lamb for one dirham. They replied, "We would not like to have it, as it is not only dead but also defective with short ears (so it was of no use even if alive)." The Prophet 🌸 then said, "This world is more insignificant to Allah than (this dead lamb) to your eye." (Sahih Muslim 7059)

Now as we walk through the lush cedars and explore the alpine meadows, let's remind ourselves to keep our tongue moist with the *dhikr* of Allah 🌸 as mentioned by our Prophet 🌸 : "Faith has seventy doors, the lowest of which is removing something harmful from a road and the highest is *la ilaha illa Allah*" (Tirmidhī 2614).

Speaking of Paradise, we know that it cannot be found in any national park, but in a way, it is under the feet of our mothers. A companion once came to the Prophet 🌸 and asked his permission to go to battle. The Prophet 🌸 asked the companion if his mother was alive. He said yes. The Prophet 🌸 replied, "Then stay with your mother, for Paradise lies beneath her feet" (Nasā'ī 3104).

9

The Flowers

And it is Allah Who sends the winds, so that they raise
up the clouds, and We drive them to a dead land, and

revive therewith the earth after its death. As such (will be)
the Resurrection!

(Al-Fāṭir 35:9)

While Denali, Yosemite, North Cascades, and Grand Teton all compete for the most perfect landscapes, the park with the most beautiful hiking trails might be Mount Rainier National Park in Washington. Covered in snow throughout the winter, the park wakes up during springtime, and the grass turns green again.

And it is He who sends the winds as heralds of glad tidings, go-
ing before His mercy (rain) until they lift up the heavy clouds.
We drive them to a dead land, then We cause water (rain)
to descend thereon. Then, We bring forth with it all sorts of
fruits. In a similar way, We will bring forth the dead. (All this
is being explained to you) so that you may learn a lesson.

(Al-A'rāf 7:57)

Mount Rainier National Park lies in the Cascade Range of the Pacific Northwest and is known for its spectacular collection of alpine wildflowers. Several hundred types of wildflowers decorate the park's meadows during spring and summer, including brilliantly colorful avalanche lilies, lupines, asters, and cinquefoil.

Wildflowers are self-seeding plants that grow naturally in the forests and play a crucial role in the forest ecosystem. The seeds either travel on animal fur or get blown away by the wind to the meadows and wetlands where they get planted. The seeds germinate, and the brightly colored flower petals attract insects who then feed on the nectar and pollen of the flower.

And We sent down blessed water (rain) from the sky, and we produced therewith gardens and grain of harvest that are reaped.
(Qāf 50:9)

As we hike Mount Rainier, it is easy for us to get distracted by its scenery. A believer, however, can use this opportunity to not only enjoy the views but also closely observe the intricate details of the flowers, how the petals are designed and shaped, the colors of the flowers, and more. Each flower's petals look so similar to each other with no defect in their making, *subhānallah*.

Have you not seen that Allah sends down water (rain) from the sky, then makes it penetrate the earth (and makes it gush forth) in the form of springs? Then He brings forth with it crops of different colors, and afterwards they wither, and you see them turn yellow; then He makes them dry and chaff. Verily, it is a lesson for the people of understanding.
(Al-Zumar 39:21)

The diversity of wildflowers is so immense that numerous books have been written on each state's specific official wildflower. Mount Rainier National Park, however, provides us the opportunity to experience an immense variety of wildflowers simultaneously. As we walk on the trail, let's close our eyes and feel the cool breeze. The wind makes the leaves rustle and spreads the sweet scent of wildflowers. We can start the *dhikr* of Allah and recite supplications to praise Him: *subhānallah, alhumdulillah, la ilaha illa Allah, Allahu Akbar*. This way, we not only join the flowers in the *dhikr* but also practice the etiquettes of the Prophet Dawud 🕊️, as mentioned by Allah ﷻ in Surah al-Anbiya.

And We subjected the mountains and the birds to glorify Our praises (Allah's purity) with Dawud. And it was We Who were the doer (of all these things).

(Al-Anbiyā' 21:79)

Subhānallah, imagine a hike where the birds, trees, and flowers join Prophet Dawud 🕊️ in the *dhikr* of Allah ﷻ. In the above āyah, Allah ﷻ is teaching us an etiquette of hiking. Everything in the forest is busy in the *dhikr* of Allah ﷻ, and the best way to appreciate the journey is to join them in the remembrance of our Lord ﷻ. Scholars have mentioned that some of the prominent Sufi dervishes of the past also had a habit of performing the *dhikr* of Allah ﷻ by going out in nature and walking in the woods. Also, the recitation of memorized surahs from the Qur'an, like Surah Al-Mulk or Surah Al-Yasin, is another way to enlighten our soul with the light of *imān.*

Surely, We bestowed grace on Dawud from Us: "O mountains, pronounce with him Allah's praise repeatedly – and you too O birds!"

(Saba' 34:10)

It is easy to get distracted by the beauty of the forest, so I personally suggest carrying prayer beads (misbaha) to remind yourself to do the *dhikr*. When we praise the One who created this beautiful world, we will feel the breeze, the plants, and the trees participating as well. The entire experience nurtures the soul, and the hike becomes a holistic spiritual session.

10

The Heat

You will certainly see Hell, then you will see it with full certitude. Then you will be asked about the pleasures (you enjoyed in the world)...

(Al-Takāthur 102:6-7)

We have appreciated the rich grasslands and floral meadows, but some areas have more activity underground than above. One such place is Kilauea, Hawai'i, in Volcanoes National Park. It is one of the most active volcanoes in the world, exuding lava continuously over the last century. There is an approximate distance of 4000 miles between the core of the earth and the surface. Hot magma rises from the core and reaches the surface as igneous rock, which takes on various forms depending on the temperature and crust conditions. The major element in volcanic rock is silica. If the magma reaches the surface as a liquid, it is called lava, which either trickles quietly or erupts violently with gases, throwing hot rocks like firebombs.

They shall enter it (Jahannam), and it is an evil place to settle in…

(Ibrāhīm 14:29)

Visiting a national park where an active volcano is erupting can frighten even an experienced traveler, but it is an exhilarating experience like no other. Hawaii's Volcanoes National

Park is a place where the magma is actively pouring out from a shield volcano that is built up from the ocean floor. Visitors hike to the Kilauea overlook at night and witness bright orange lava ejecting from the core of the earth. The site is incredibly photogenic but also a stark reminder of reality. We not only see the volcano but also feel its heat under our feet. Imagine the hot lava of *Jahannam* and the extreme heat, which will be seventy times hotter than anything in this world. May Allah protect us from the hellfire. The Prophet ﷺ warned us about the hellfire, saying, "the fire of this world is one part from seventy parts of the fire of Hell" (Tirmidhī 2590).

Looking at the erupting volcano, imagine the day of resurrection when *Jahannam* will be in front of us, and we all will have to pass on the bridge of the *sirāt*. Imagine how many people will end up falling into the fire of Jahannam and what a frightful sight it will be for everyone. *Astaghfirullah.*

Surely, those who have disbelieved in Our verses, We shall certainly make them enter a fire. Whenever their skins are burnt out, We shall give them other skins in their place,

that they may taste the punishment. Surely, Allah is Ever Most Powerful, All-Wise.

(Al-Nisā' 4:56)

There is much to say about the size and features of a volcano, but to look at it without the lens of *imān* is truly a loss.

Another of the largest volcanoes in the world is at the Lassen Volcanic National Park, California. It belongs to the "plug dome" category of volcanoes, where the lava does not flow far from the source. This volcano last erupted in 1915, and nobody except Allah ﷻ knows when the next eruption will take place. Maybe it will happen during the Last Hour, when everything on earth will be reduced to flat land, and Allah knows best.

Then, once the trumpet will be blown for the first time, and the earth and the mountains will be lifted and crushed into pieces with a single blow, then on that day the Happening will happen, and the sky will burst apart, while it will have become frail on that day.

(Al-Ḥaqqah 69:13-16)

No! When the earth will be crushed thoroughly to be turned into bits...

(Al-Fajr 89:21)

Some volcanoes do not remain hot forever, instead become calm and soothing lakes. Allah ﷻ has given us one such example at the Crater Lake National Park, a place like no other, and the deepest lake in the U.S. The water is so blue that one cannot help but feel calm and serene just by looking at it. The remarkably clear water of the lake allows the sunlight to penetrate deeper, so that longer wavelengths of light are absorbed and shorter wavelengths such as blue light are reflected on the surface, turning the lake deep blue in color. The contrast of the evergreen pine trees makes the landscape even more beautiful. Looking at the perfect landscape, it is hard to believe that the entire region was once rocked by volcanic activity. Geologists postulate that about 7000 years ago the earth's crustal plane collision resulted in a violent volcanic eruption that emptied the volcanic chamber of magma, ash, and trapped gases. The mountain thus collapsed, and the large area over time was filled with rainwater and snow. Another fascinating fact about Crater Lake is that it does not give rise to any streams or rivers. Here, the water system is balanced just by evaporation and seepage. The water is some of the purest on earth, with only 79 toxic particles per million, *subhānallah*. In contrast, the Great Salt Lake in Utah, also lacking any connecting rivers, contains the second saltiest water on the planet.

And the two seas are not alike; this one is sweet, saturating, pleasant to drink, and that one is salty, bitter.

(Fāṭir 35:12)

The system of our planet is run perfectly by the Divine power of Allah ﷻ. He has placed deep knowledge for us in nature if only we observe it closely.

Verily! in the creation of the heavens and the earth, and in the alternation of night and day, there are signs for the people of wisdom, those who remember Allah standing and sitting, and (lying) on their sides, and ponder on the creation of the heavens and the earth (and say), "Our Lord, You have not created all this without purpose. We proclaim Your glory, so save us from the punishment of the Fire..."

(Āali-ʿImrān 3:190–191)

Some of the parks we visited have beauty that reminded us of *Jannah*, and some have fires that reminded us of *Jahannam*, but are there any parks that might show us both at the same time? Yellowstone National Park is where we find our answer.

Visitors from all around the world come to Yellowstone to see the tall waterfalls and the world-famous Old Faithful geyser. Spread over 2.2 million acres of Wyoming, Montana, and Idaho, it provides a perfect blend of snow-covered glaciers, canyons, and thermal hot springs in one place. Constant

crustal movements at Yellowstone explain the park's unique geothermal activity. Walking near the mammoth hot springs and the geyser basins, one can appreciate the colors of the dynamic hydrothermal system and feel the superheated water fumes evaporating from them, the bubbling of the mud pots and the pungent gases, sulfuric acid, and hydrogen sulfide. The steam continues to erupt even through heavy snowfall in the winter's subfreezing temperatures, turning into clouds which then release even more snow, *subhānallah*.

For a believer, Yellowstone is a perfect place to remember the greatness of Allah 🌸. The cold water of the river and the scalding liquid of the geysers stay within their boundaries and obey Allah 🌸. People do not like to think about their death when they are on vacation, but remembering the departure from this world is one of the fastest ways to bring the consciousness of Allah 🌸 into our hearts. The beauty of Yellowstone National Park is temporary: all of it will be turned into dust one day, as our Prophet 🌸 mentioned: "Frequently remember the destroyer of pleasures, meaning death" (Ibn Mājah 4258).

And say, "The truth is from you Lord. Now, whosoever wills may believe and whosoever wills may deny." Verily, We have prepared for the wrongdoers a fire whose walls will envelope them. And if they will beg for help, they shall be helped with water like boiling oil that will scald the faces. Terrible is the drink, and evil is the Fire as a resting place.

(Al-Kahf 18:29)

The hissing steam vents and hot geysers of Yellowstone remind us of the hot liquids of *Jahannam* (may Allah protect us from it).Walking on the boardwalk at the geyser basin trail, we protect ourselves from the boiling water of geysers. One may suffer from severe burns and scalding if one falls into it. When looking at the geysers, let's pray to Allah ﷻ to protect us from the torment of the grave and the Hellfire. The Prophet ﷺ used to pray, "I take refuge in Allah from the Hellfire; woe to the inmates of the Hellfire!" (Abū Dāwūd 881).

The Prophet ﷺ said: "When a human is laid in his grave and his companions return back, he hears their footsteps. Two angels come to him and make him sit and ask: 'What did you say about Muhammad?' The man will say: 'I testify that he is Allah's slave and His Prophet.' The angels will say, 'Look at your place in the Hellfire, Allah has given you a place in Heaven instead.' The angels will show him both hellfire and heaven. But a disbeliever will not be able to answer the question and the angels will say to him, 'Neither did you know, nor did you take the guidance (from the Qur'an).' He will be hit with an iron hammer between his two ears. He will cry and the cry will be heard by whatever approaches him except the humans and jinns." (Bukhārī 1338)

The purpose of remembering the hellfire and death while traveling is not to be paralyzed by a state of fear, but rather to remember the temporary nature of our life, which may end at any moment. The reminder of the Hereafter controls our *nafs* (ego) and protects our souls from getting lost in the shallow, short-lived luxuries of this world.

May Allah ﷻ make us amongst those who will be given their record in the right hand, *ameen.*

And you (all) will be in three kinds (separate groups). So those on the Right Hand (those who will be given their

Records in their right hand), who will be those on the Right Hand? (As a respect for them because they will enter Paradise). And those on the Left Hand (those who will be given their Record in their left hand), who will be those on the Left Hand? (As a disgrace for them because they will enter the hellfire). And those foremost (in faith) will be foremost (in the Hereafter). Those are the ones brought near (to Allah).

(Al-Waqi'ah 56:7-11)

11

The sky

We made the sky a protected roof; yet they turn away

from its signs.

(Al-Anbiyā' 21:32)

G *ive them the example of the life of this world; it is like water (rain) We sent down from the sky, then the vegetation of the earth was mingled with it, and then it turned fresh and green. But (later) it becomes dry and broken pieces that are blown by the winds, and Allah is powerful over everything.*

(Al-Kahf 18:45)

Bright and blue during the day and dark and sparkling at night, the sky is one of the great signs of Allah's supremacy. It is vast and perfect, fulfilling its role given by Allah ﷻ. Sometimes decorated with clouds and other times pale and pink, the sky looks beautiful no matter the time of day. There is no hole or imperfection in the exquisiteness of the sky. It is mentioned beautifully in Surah Mulk:

...Who has created seven skies, one over the other. You will see nothing out of proportion in the creation of the Rahmān (the All-Merciful Allah). Then look again, do you see any rifts?

(Al-Mulk 67: 3-4)

In the sky we often see clouds made from water and ice crystals, through which Allah ﷻ blesses us with rain and snow. Rain is a blessing from Allah; however, sometimes, we find a negative attitude toward monsoons in the West. Intense rain due to global warming may indeed become problematic, but as Muslims, we must never curse the rainfall. Instead, we should pray to Allah to make it beneficial for us.

Again, tell Me about the water you drink: Is it you who has brought it down from the clouds, or are We the One who sends (it) down? If We so will, We can make it bitter in taste. So why do you not offer gratitude?

(Al-Wāqiʿah 56:68-70)

Rainwater is rich in minerals crucial for the growth of vegetation and the ecological balance of the planet.

And We sent down blessed water (rain) from the sky and caused to grow therewith gardens and grain of harvest that are reaped.

(Qāf 50:9)

The clouds that store rain are also the source of lightning that may ignite fires in our forests. Interestingly, even lightning is necessary for us, as it stabilizes the electrical balance in our atmosphere and supports ozone production. Even the fires that seem destructive to us are sometimes necessary to enrich the soil with minerals.

Do you not realize that Allah drives the clouds gently, then joins them together, then turns them into a heap of layers? Then you see the rain comes forth from between them. He sends down from the sky mountains (of clouds) having hail in them, then He strikes therewith whom He wills and turns it away from whom He wills. The vivid flash of its lightning nearly blinds the sight.

(Al-Nūr 24:43)

Forest fires are a natural part of recycling dead vegetation and avoiding overaccumulation. They create space for seeds to germinate, kill insects, and control overgrowth in the forest. The burnt ash is recycled into new soil for the trees. Allah ﷻ has designed the forest in a way that everything is recycled.

The section on the beauty of the sky is not complete without mentioning stars. They, too, are busy in the *dhikr* of Allah 🕮, just like plants, trees, and animals.

Have you not seen that whoever is in the heavens and whoever is on the earth, and the sun, and the moon, and the stars, and the mountains, the trees, the animals, and many of mankind prostrate themselves to Allah? But there are many on whom punishment has become due. And the one whom Allah puts to disgrace, there is no one to give him respect. Verily, Allah does what He wills.

(Al-Ḥajj 22:18)

Notice the meteors, or "shooting stars". These are pieces of rock that heat up and fall into the earth's atmosphere. Some in the West have come to think of them as good omens, but Allah 🕮 has explained the phenomenon in the Qur'an:

Verily, We have decorated the nearest sky with an adornment, the stars, and (have made them) a security against every rebellious devil. They cannot listen to the Upper Realm and are hit from every side to be driven off, and for them there is a lasting punishment; however, if one snatches a little bit, he is pursued by a bright flame.

(Al- Ṣāffāt 37: 6-10)

As we notice the sky, think about the amount of knowledge given to mankind by Allah 🕌. Today, humans can fly out of the atmosphere and explore the constellations and galaxies. We have collected rocks from the moon, displayed at the NASA Space Center in Houston, Texas, and are trying to grow vegetation on Mars. There was, however, a human being who went beyond everyone else, about 1400 years ago, and he was shown all the seven skies. Let's remind ourselves of the night of *Mirāj*, when the Prophet 🕌 was taken on a journey through the heavens. Ibn Abbas narrated: "The sights which were shown to the Prophet 🕌 on the Night Journey (of *Mirāj*) when he was taken to *Bayt al-Maqdis* (Jerusalem) were actual sights (not dreams). And the cursed tree (mentioned) in the Qur'an is the tree of *Zaqqum* (a bitter pungent tree that grows at the bottom of Hell)." (Bukhārī 4716)

Allah is the One who made for you the earth a place to live, and the sky a roof, and shaped you, and made your shapes so good – and provided you with a lot of good things. That is Allah, your Lord. So Glorious is Allah, the Lord of the worlds.
(Al-Mu'min 40:64)

...and sent down water from the heavens and revived the land with it after it was dead. Surely, in that there is a sign for people who listen.
(Al-Naḥl 16:65)

The national parks in the northern hemisphere are known for the northern lights, the aurora borealis, which appear every winter. Voyageurs National Park in Minnesota or remote areas in Alaska provide some of the best views. The reasoning for the northern lights is fascinating, and Allah ﷻ has blessed us with the knowledge of geophysics to understand it. Around the planet earth is a magnetic field called the magnetosphere whose function is to protect us from charged particles. Charged particles that reach the earth's surface are repelled by the magnetic field, and the process of repulsion and the movement of photons create the northern lights. Allah ﷻ has mentioned this phenomenon in the Qur'an, *subhānallah*:

So, I swear by the twilight (afterglow of sunset), and by the night and whatever it gathers in its darkness...

(Al-Inshiqāq 84:16-17)

Once we understand the verses in the Qur'an about our galaxy, celestial objects carry even more meaning than we previously realized.

12

The beauty of the colors

Did you not see that Allah has sent down water (rain) from the sky? Then We produce therewith fruits having different

> *colors. And among the mountains there are streaks, white*
> *and red – of different colors, and (others) utterly black.*
>
> *(Fāṭir 35:27)*

In the above *āyah*, Allah 🕌 mentions some geological colors. Some mountains have such unique shades of color that
they look like canvas paintings. The mountains of Badlands
National Park of South Dakota are one such example. These
mountains get their red and white colors from erosion and
deposition of elements: red from the oxidation of iron and an
orange-pink color from limestone and selenite. Paleontologists
discovered in this region fossils of elephants and mammoths,
another reminder that our temporary life must end one day. The
question is, are we ready to go back to our Lord? As our Prophet 🕌 said, "Frequently remember the destroyer of pleasures,
death" (Ibn Mājah 4258).

When we visit the national parks, we sometimes get to meet
hikers who are sunrise enthusiasts. We can spot a photographer
hiking early in the morning to catch a glimpse of the very first
sun rays on the mountains. The rising of the sun is one of the

most beautiful times of the day, and when we observe it, let's remind ourselves that the sun is coming back to work after taking permission from Allah ﷻ. A day will come when this permission will not be granted. One day, the Prophet ﷺ asked his companion Abu Dhar ؓ if he knew where the sun goes at the time of sunset. Abu Dhar ؓ replied, "Allah and His Prophet know better." The Prophet ﷺ then explained to him, "The sun prostrates under the Throne and takes permission to rise again. A time will come (near the end) when permission will not be granted, and the sun will be asked to return and so it will rise from the west." (Bukhārī 3199)

We must note that the Prophet ﷺ mentioned the movement of the sun in the context of how things look to us from the earth and not how they really exist. The word "prostration" may also imply the obedience and *dhikr* of Allah by every creature in the universe, including the sun, but we are not able to understand it.

Have you not seen that whoever is in the heavens and whoever is on the earth, and the sun, and the moon, and the stars, and the mountains, the trees, the animals, and many of mankind prostrate themselves to Allah? But there are many on whom punishment has become due. And the one whom Allah puts to disgrace, there is no one to give him respect. Verily, Allah does what He wills.

(Al-Ḥajj 22:18)

As the dawn breaks and the sunbeams fall on the Badlands of South Dakota, we get to see hundreds of colors, most of which do not even have a name yet. Another place where the beauty of the sunrise is evident is at the Black Canyon of Gunnison National Park in Colorado, one of the most underrated national parks in the country. In the morning, the pitch-black canyons are woken up by the sun, and as the light falls on them, we enjoy a picturesque sight of the giant canyons changing their colors, from black to purple with a pinkish hue. The entire park, including the wildlife, wakes up and embraces the new day as a fresh start.

All the seven skies and the earth and all those therein extol His glory. And there is not a single thing that does not extol His glory, but you do not understand their extolling. Surely, He is Forbearing, Most-Forgiving.

(Banī Isrā'īl 17: 44)

Every morning Allah ﷻ gives us the chance to rectify our matters, to do His *dhikr* and perform our prayers with more focus. Every day we are given the opportunity to be grateful for the eyes that see this world, the lungs that can still breathe, and the heart that is still alive with the remembrance of Allah ﷻ. What a loss it would be to witness the sunrise and not praise the One who is glorified by all.

Did you not see that Allah makes the night enter into the day, and makes the day enter into the night (the decrease in the hours of the night is added to the hours of the day), and He has subjected the sun and the moon, each running its course towards an appointed time, and that Allah is fully aware of what you do?

(Luqmān 31:29)

The rising of the sun every morning is a great blessing. There are places in the world where it remains dark for several months at a time, in Scandinavian countries and the North Pole. Therefore, when observing the quiet sunrise in a national park, we can take time to appreciate the significance of the sun and the blessings of Allah ﷻ everywhere around us.

Allah alternates the night and the day to succeed each other. Truly, in this there is a lesson for those who have insight.
(Al-Nūr 24:44)

May Allah ﷻ make us amongst the grateful ones, *ameen*.

13

The animals of the national parks

There is no creature moving (living) on the earth, nor a bird flying on its two wings, except that they are communities like you. We have not missed anything in the book. Then, to their Lord they (all) shall be gathered.

(Al-An'ām 6:38)

The national parks are a good place to observe not only the sky and the flora but also the wildlife. Allah ﷻ created a diverse environment on this planet where He provides *rizq* to all the creatures. It is of course not possible to mention or even know every living being, but we can talk about the animals who live inside the national parks.

Allah 🌟 is the *Razzāq* (Provider) and upon Him is the provision of all His living beings. From the bats of Carlsbad Caverns to the whales at Channel Islands National Park, all animals are satiated by the time they go to sleep at night. Animals, unlike humans, usually do not store their food but wake up in the morning and get busy with the *dhikr* of Allah 🌟 and are provided with *rizq*. It is narrated that the Prophet 🌟 said: "If you were to rely upon Allah with the required reliance, then He would provide for you just as a bird is provided for: it goes out in the morning empty and returns full at dusk" (Tirmidhī 2344).

The animals are dependent on each other for their needs and share an ecological community. Everglades National Park is an example of a place where the tropical and the temperate species flourish together. It is an international biosphere reserve and home of freshwater otters, softshell turtles, tricolored heron, white-tailed deer, and many more, living together in harmony. The Everglades is also known to be the only place in the world where alligators and crocodiles coexist together in the wild. Wind Cave National Park in South Dakota is another haven where bison, prairie dogs, and pronghorns thrive on land, and underneath the prairie lies a cave system where thousands of bats have their homes.

The giant grizzly bears of Katmai National Park in Alaska are fed with abundant salmon from the Brooks River, so much that the bear acquires five inches of subcutaneous fat by winter. The preparation for hibernation starts as the winter approaches, and the bears sleep for the next five months. Their body temperature goes low, their appetite is suppressed, and the animal does not urinate throughout this period. Allah ﷻ created a special system in the bodies of hibernating animals. During hibernation, the animal metabolizes fat instead of protein to obtain energy for body function. As a result, minimal urea is produced which then recycles back to make protein. Thus, the bear does not make urine (protection against dehydration) and retains muscle mass at the same time. Along with this, the animal remains asleep for months but does not develop any pressure sores, *subhānallah*.

Hibernation is not just for bigger animals, but also for smaller ones, such as the mice of White Sand Dunes National Park. The

Apache pocket mouse, known for its fur pockets on its cheeks, thrives on seeds and insects. They also hibernate in winter, and their kidneys easily survive without water for months.

The Qur'an enlightens us with two stories where Allah ﷻ gave a long hibernating period to humans. One is in Surah al-Kahf where the People of the Cave slept for about three hundred years. The other is in Surah al-Baqarah where we learn about Prophet Uzair ﷺ, who was kept asleep for one hundred years.

Or, (do you not know) the example of the one who passed by a town that had collapsed on its roofs. He said: "How shall Allah bring it to life after it is dead?" So, Allah caused him to die for a hundred years, then raised him saying: "How long did you remain (in this state)?" He (the man) said: "(Perhaps) I remained (dead) for a day or part of a day." He said: "Nay, you have remained (dead) for a hundred years; look at your food and your drink, it has not spoiled. Now look at your donkey. (We did) this to make you a sign for people! Look at the bones, how We bring them together, then dress them with flesh." When it was clear to him, he said: "I know (now) that Allah is Powerful over everything."

(Al-Baqarah 2:259)

When it comes to birds, a wide range of species make their homes in the national parks. Some of the most iconic ones include the bald eagle in Kenai Fjords National Park in Alaska, Hawaiian Petrel in the Volcanoes National Park, and Clark's Nutcracker in the Yosemite National Park. The study of birds and their body adaptations is a vast topic, still not fully understood by humans. How small birds regulate their body temperature and survive the bitter cold of Yellowstone, and continue to find their *rizq*, is an astonishing process that points towards the greatness of Allah ﷻ.

Do they not see the birds held (flying) in the midst of the sky? No one holds them but Allah. Verily, in that there are signs for a people who believe.

(Al-Naḥl 16:79)

The above animals are just a few examples of how the life cycle continues in the wild. But we do not have to go to a forest to observe the remarkable fauna in our ecosystem. A small fish in an aquarium is as unique as a grizzly bear in Alaska. All we need is vision and understanding that praises the unfathomable knowledge of the Lord.

14

The most incredible park

*And Allah created you from dust, then from a sperm-drop;
then He made you mates. And no female conceives, nor does
she give birth except with His knowledge. And no aged*

person is granted (additional) life nor is his lifespan lessened but that is in a register. Indeed, that for Allah is easy.

(Al-Fāṭir 35:11)

Forests and the national parks broaden our horizons and give us the chance to observe Allah's ﷻ creativity. They remind us about the significance of the *dhikr* of Allah ﷻ and His power. But there is a park which is the most beautiful of all. It is more beautiful than the sun, the moon, and the stars, and that national park is the human body. Allah ﷻ places His mercy on all creatures, and He loves humans the most. All plants and animals are made to provide service to mankind.

We have created man in the best composition (mould)…
(Al-Ttn 95:4)

Our existence starts from a drop of liquid. A completely new human body with organs including the heart, lungs, and kidneys is made out of a single drop.

Verily, We have created man from a mixed semen-drop in order to try him; then We made him able to hear, able to see.
(Al-Dahr 76:2)

As soon as the newborn baby takes the first breath, the circulatory method and the breathing techniques are altered. The body that relied on its mother's blood for all its needs now breathes on its own, seconds after arriving in the world.

The more we learn about the human body, the more we must praise the greatness of Allah ﷻ. We have similar organs on the inside, yet our DNA makeup and physical features are different. Not even the two eyes are the same. The blood vessels running through our body are about 60,000 miles long. The muscles in our limbs are different from the ones in our heart. Our heart is constantly pumping blood and has the strongest muscles in our body.

Allah's creativity is not limited to the organs that we can see with the naked eye. He has also blessed us with a complex system not otherwise visible without the help of a microscope, i.e., the immune system. Our immunity protects us from harmful pathogens and environmental toxins. It is fascinating to know that the human body is constantly producing cancer, but not everyone is affected by it. This is because of the excellent DNA repair enzyme system, an immune surveillance system, which is busy auditing DNA and killing cells with defective DNA. Health is a special blessing from Allah ﷻ, and we should always be grateful to Allah ﷻ for it.

(Recall the time) when your Lord declared, "If you express gratitude, I shall certainly give you more, and if you are ungrateful, then My punishment is severe."
(Ibrāhīm 14:7)

At this time, as we are reading this book, there is an entire system of organs in our body, working silently and performing duties given by Allah ﷻ, starting from our eyes that are reading this book, detecting colors, and transferring the signals to the brain. The brain then recognizes the words and sends the signal to the eyes to keep reading. Millions of neurons in the brain are also controlling our hands, making us think, and storing the memory all at once. The heart is constantly beating from the time we take our first breath and is pumping blood to the entire body, not leaving a single area without circulation. The lungs are breathing air in and out without us realizing that millions of alveoli are constantly oxygenating our blood. When we eat, about 80,000 taste buds on our tongue provide the taste. As the food goes inside, the stomach digests it and the intestines absorb the nutrients from it. Our liver is busy detoxifying the chemicals, and our kidneys are filtering out waste from the body. Our urine, which contains toxins, is made in the body and passes through the ureters to get stored in the bladder. The urine, however, never clogs the ureters, and this is due to the massive surge of an enzyme called urokinase that does not let the urine clot.

These are only the basics of a human body, and Allah ﷻ has kept many intricate details that we cannot even imagine. It takes years to become a physician and then several more years to specialize in a certain field—for example, four years of training to be an ophthalmologist and two more years to specialize in the retina. Unfortunately, we usually only realize the significance of this body when we are sick.

And indeed, We have honored the children of Adam and We have carried them on the land and in the sea (provided rides) and provided them with lawful good things and made them much superior to many of those whom We have created.

(Banī Isrā'īl 17:70)

Remembering the blessings of Allah 🌸 and saying *shukr* and *istighfār* is the way to attain a level of tranquility that no park in this world can provide. Allah 🌸 has blessed us with a healthy body, and it is our responsibility to take care of it by eating well and staying active.

As we travel through the national parks, let's remember the blessings of Allah 🌸 upon us. Say *shukr* for the eyes that can see the natural beauty created by Allah, for the legs that help us do the strenuous hikes, for the arms that support the body and enable us to do our work. Say *shukr* for the lungs that are benefiting from our deep breaths and for the heart that powers us as we hike, for the kidneys that preserve the water when we get dehydrated on the trails.

Most importantly, let's be grateful to Allah ﷻ for giving us another day to praise Him, to rectify our mistakes through *tawba* and *istaghfār*.

May Allah also make us enjoy the beautiful landscapes of *Jannah* as He did for this world.

Jabir ibn Abdullah narrated that he heard the Prophet ﷺ say: "The best of remembrance is *la ilaha illa Allah* (none has the right to be worshipped but Allah), and the best of supplication is *alhamdulillah* (praise is to Allah)" (Ibn Mājah 3800).

Conclusion

*And no person can ever die except by Allah's leave and at
an appointed term. And whoever desires a reward in (this)
world, We shall give him of it; and whoever desires a reward*

in the Hereafter, We shall give him thereof. And We shall
reward the grateful.

(Al-Imran 3:145)

While some may think that the reminder of death and the day of *Qiyāmah* would make their exploration of the woods less enjoyable, the truth is, nature is created by Allah ﷻ so that we think about Him when we observe it. Nature reminds us of the departure from this temporary world and the life in the Hereafter. Allah ﷻ has asked us in the Qur'an to explore the world, and the purpose of that is to bring our heart to the remembrance of Allah ﷻ; after all, this is what we are created for.

Abu Huraira ﷺ narrated that the Prophet ﷺ once mentioned: "Allah ﷻ has mobile (squads) of angels, who have no other work (to attend to but) to follow the assemblies of *dhikr* of Allah ﷻ, and when they find such assemblies, they sit in them and some of them surround the others with their wings till the space between them and the sky of the world is fully covered, and when the assembly of *dhikr* is adjourned, they go upward to heaven. Allah 🕮, the Exalted and Glorious, asks them (although He is best informed about them): 'Where have you come from?' The angels say: 'We come from Your servants upon the earth who had been glorifying You (reciting *subhānallah*), declaring Your Greatness and Oneness (saying *Allāhu Akbar* and *la ilaha illa Allah*) and praising You (by saying *alhamdulillah*) and asking from You.' Allah 🕮 says: 'What do they ask from Me?' They say: 'They ask for Paradise.' Allah 🕮 says: 'Have they seen My Paradise?' They say, 'No, our Lord.' Allah 🕮 says: 'What if they were to see My Paradise?' The angels say: 'They seek Your protection.' Allah 🕮 says: 'From what do they seek My protection?' They say: 'From Your Hellfire, our Lord.' Allah 🕮 says: 'Have they seen my Hellfire?' They say: 'No, our Lord.' Allah 🕮 says: 'What if they were to see My Hellfire?' They say: 'They ask for Your Forgiveness.' Allah 🕮 says: 'I will pardon them, give them what they request, and grant them protection.' They say: 'Our Lord, there is one among them, a simple servant who happened to pass by and sit there alongside them.' Allah 🕮 says: 'I will also grant him pardon, for whoever sits with these fellows will not suffer misery.'" (Bukhari 6408)

May Allah makes us amongst those whose minds remember Him always. May He bless our soul with the light of *imān* and provide us with two friends, *duā* and *shukr* (supplication and gratitude), that keep us connected to him always, ameen.

He created the heavens and earth in truth and formed you and perfected your forms; and to Him is the (final) destination.

(Al-Taghābun 64:3)

List the names of your favorite scenic areas or places you would like to visit. (Do not forget to take this book with you on your next trip.)

_____

_____

_____

_____

_____

_____

_____

_____

_____

_____

_____

List the different kinds of dhikr you are planning to include on your next hike. (If you'd like, you can share the photo of your list with your online review of this book, to motivate others.)

_____

_____

_____

_____

_____

_____

_____

_____

_____

_____

_____

_____

What extraordinary components of nature did you notice on your hike? (Trees, rocks, mushrooms, animals, etc.)

_____

_____

_____

_____

_____

_____

_____

_____

_____

_____

_____

What are you most grateful for during your trip to the national or state parks?

_____

_____

_____

_____

_____

_____

_____

_____

_____

_____

_____

Which of the sunnahs of our Prophet ﷺ did you revive in your recent nature travels?

_____

_____

_____

_____

_____

_____

_____

_____

_____

_____

_____

_____

List your favorite scenic byways and hiking trails, or places you want to see on your next trip. (Don't forget to share this list with your friends!)

Glossary

Jalla Jalāluhu - may His glory be Glorified

Sallallāhu 'alayhi wasallam - may Allah bless him and give him peace

Raḍiyallāhu 'anhu - may Allah be pleased with him

Raḍiyallāhu 'anha - may Allah be pleased with her

'Alayhi al-salām - peace be upon him

Ar-Rahmān-the name and attribute of Allah, means The Most Merciful

Ar-Raheem - the name and attribute of Allah, means The Most Compassionate

Akhira - the Hereafter

Alhumdulillah - praise be to Allah Allāhu Akbar - Allah is the greatest

Al-Hijr - Hegra, an archaeological site in Saudi Arabia

As'hāb e Kahf - companions of the cave Astaghfirullah - I seek Allah's forgiveness

Āyah - a verse in the Qur'an

Bayt al-Maqdis - al-Aqsa Mosque in Jerusalem

Dhikr - remembrance of Allah

Duā - prayer/ supplication

Deen - way of life/religion

Glossary

La Ilaha Illa Allah - there is no God but Allah

Mashā'Allāh - what Allah wills

Mi'rāj - the night when Prophet Muhammad ﷺ ascent to the Heavens

Hidāyah - guidance

Hadith - a saying from Prophet Muhammad ﷺ

Qiyāmah - the day of resurrection

Rizq - sustenance

Sadaqah - voluntary charity

Salah - mandatory prayer for Muslims

Sirāt - the bridge over hell

Shūkr - thankfulness and gratitude Subhānallah - all praise be to
Allah Surah - a chapter in the Qur'an

Sadaqā jāriyah - a voluntary charity that benefits people long-
term even after death

Taqwā - consciousness of Allah

Tabūk - a city in the northwestern region of Saudi Arabia

Acknowledgements

*A*lhamdulillah, praise be to Allah ﷺ who chose me to be the author of this book. When devising a manuscript, a human mind can only plan on writing it. The execution of the plan and the flow of the words comes only from Allah ﷺ. When we intend it for a noble cause, Allah ﷺ sends help from sources we can never imagine. Such was the case with this book. A team of experts helped me throughout my journey in writing this manuscript. This includes my copyeditor Cyrus McGoldrick, the illustrator Ashley Limbaugh, the formatting designer Jessica Cameron, and the cover designer, Sheeba Sheikh. Of course, the entire journey to the national parks and then writing about them would not have been possible without the two strong pillars in my life, my parents. I am thankful to them for giving me the strength of education, the spirit of adventure, and for always making *duā* for me. I am also grateful to the U.S. National Park Service for answering my queries and sending me educational materials on the history and geology of the national parks.

Lastly, I would like to thank all my readers who gave me their most valuable asset, their time, and read this book. May Allah ﷻ make this book a source of *sadaqah jariya* that not only benefits us in this life but also in *akhirah, ameen*.

Notes

Drori J., Around the world in 80 plants, London, Laurence King Publishing, 2021.

Hassan K, Hussain NHM, Akhir NM, et al., 'Plants, Landscape and Architecture: Stories from the Quran, J Appl. Environ. Biol. Sci, 7(IS)21-26, 2017.

Harris AG, Tuttle E., Geology of National Parks, Fourth Edition, Dubuque, Kendall/Hunt Publishing, 1990.

Huikari O, Trees and how they work, San Rafael, Wooden Books, 2021

Ibrahim MA., Mountains as stabilizers for earth from the Quranic and modern science perspectives. IJASOS, 5(15), 2019.

Jose S, Trees, Leaves, Flowers & Seeds, Penguin Random House, New York, 2019

Knighton C, Leave only footprints, New York, Crown Publishing, 2020.

Pitts C, USA's National Parks, Lonely Planet, 2016.

Pak Peaks, 8 July 2017. <http://www.pakpeaks.com/2017/07/08/holy-quran-and-mountains/>, accessed 20 January 2022.

Thajuddin, K.S., Water in the Quran, Linkedin, 7 October 2019. https://www.linkedin.com/pulse/water-quran-kulsanofer-syed-thajudeen-phd/, accessed 26 February 2022.

Wohlleben P, The hidden life of trees, Munich, Greystone Books, 2015

Further Reading

Around the World in 80 Trees by Jonathan Drori

Around the World in 80 Plants by Jonathan Drori

Birds: Their Life, Their Ways, Their World by Reader's Digest Association

Forest Meditations by Stephen Joseph

Forest Bathing Retreat by Hannah Fries

Geology of National Parks by Ann G. Harris and Esther Tuttle

How to Be More Trees by Annie Davidson

Leave Only Footprints by Conor Knighton

Nature Anatomy by Julia Rothman

Our National Parks by John Muir

Scenic Science of the National Parks by Emily Hoff

The Inner Life of Animals by Peter Wohlleben

The Secret Wisdom of Nature by Peter Wohlleben

The Best Coast, a Road Trip Atlas by Chandler O'Leary

Trees and How They Work by Olavi Huikari

The Secret Life of Fish by Doug Mackay – Hope

The Social Lives of Animals by Ashley Ward

The Great Alaska Nature Factbook by Susan Ewing

Tip of the Iceberg by Mark Adams

World of Wonders by Aimee Nezhukumatathil

About the author

Abeer Arain, M.D., M.P.H., is a physician, a traveler, and a gardener. She is a Hematologist and Medical Oncologist in Idaho, United States. When not practicing medicine, she can be found working in her garden, planning her next hike, or browsing her local bookstore. She is passionate about exploring the backcountry and national parks and loves to connect nature with the remembrance of Allah ﷻ and the stories of the Prophets.

Index